Action! In the Classroom

A Guide to Student Produced Digital Video in K–12 Education

Daniel R. Greenwood

Rowman & Littlefield Education
Lanham • New York • Toronto • Oxford
2003

This title was originally published by ScarecrowEducation. First Rowman & Littlefield Education edition 2005.

Published in the United States of America
by Rowman & Littlefield Education
A Division of Rowman & Littlefield Publishers, Inc.
A wholly owned subsidiary of The Rowman & Littlefield Publishing Group, Inc.
4501 Forbes Boulevard, Suite 200, Lanham, Maryland 20706
www.rowmaneducation.com

PO Box 317
Oxford
OX2 9RU, UK

British Library Cataloguing in Publication Information Available

Library of Congress Cataloging-in-Publication Data

Greenwood, Daniel R. (Daniel Robert), 1969–
  Action! in the classroom : a guide to student produced digital
video in K–12 education / Daniel R. Greenwood.
      p. cm.—"A ScarecrowEducation book."
  Includes bibliographical references (p.   ) and index.
  ISBN 0-8108-4662-4 (pbk. : alk. paper)
      1. Video tapes in education—Handbooks, manuals, etc. 2. Video
recordings—Production and direction—Handbooks, manuals, etc. 3.
Project method in teaching—Handbooks, manuals, etc. I. Title.
LB1044.75 .G75 2003
371.33'523—dc21

                                            2002151861

♾™ The paper used in this publication meets the minimum requirements of American National Standard for Information Sciences—Permanence of Paper for Printed Library Materials, ANSI/NISO Z39.48-1992. Manufactured in the United States of America.

To Beth, my wonderful, supporting, and loving wife.

Contents

Part IV   Media Literacy

Appendix

Acknowledgments

Many talented people gave generously of their time and talents to make this book a reality. Several people reviewed every page, and their comments and suggestions improved the text immensely.

I would like to start by thanking my family. Most of all I want to thank my wife, Beth, not only for acting as my initial proofreader, but also for supporting me during the many months of the planning and writing of the book. My sister, Kim Van Horn; mother, Janet Greenwood; and father, Rob Cowgill, diligently read, corrected, and made suggestions on every chapter, and I owe them a great deal of gratitude.

I want to thank my colleagues at St. Catherine's, most especially Howard Pugh, who spent many hours reading and editing everything from the book proposal to the completed manuscript. Howard's many editorial suggestions and superb comments improved the book substantially. I also want to thank my Technology Department colleagues George Ludden, Chris Brown, and Thomas Bannard, whose expertise and creativity I relied on heavily, as usual.

I would like to thank Dr. John Bunch, my teacher and advisor at the University of Virginia, for introducing me to video production and its educational potential. His expertise and support are greatly appreciated. I would also like to thank Will Davis, under whose tutelage much of the manuscript was completed.

Many readers reviewed portions of the book and made excellent recommendations and expressed positive support. They are: Dr. Alan Bain, Cathy McGehee, Patrick Loach, Patty Sauls, and Rita Root.

I also want to thank St. Catherine's School; Gussie Bannard, head of school; and Jackie Wilkins, assistant head of school, for supporting my efforts to integrate new technology into our excellent curriculum—through formal coursework, classroom implementations, and financial support of the Technology Department. I would also like to thank Pam Roberts and Barbara Robertson for their initiative, expertise, and enthusiasm on some of my initial educational video collaborations.

Finally, I would like to thank Cindy Tursman and ScarecrowEducation Press for giving me an opportunity to publish this book and Bevin McLaughlin for such a thorough job of editing the text.

Introduction

STUDENT PRODUCED VIDEO IN EDUCATION

Video is an extremely powerful and sophisticated form of communication that has changed our culture and continues to have a profound effect on our society. Students' choices in fashion, music, and behavior are heavily influenced by the personalities, advertisements, and information they see on television and at the movies. The video medium has more impact on modern students than any other form of mass communication.

The potential to exploit this medium for educational benefit is immense. When broken down, video is simply a communication medium used to inform, entertain, persuade, tell a story, and/or express oneself. The ability to communicate a message to an audience is one of the most important skills we teach our students. We strive to teach this skill through writing, projects, public speaking, drama, fine and performing arts. Adding video production to the list gives our students a new means of expression, employing the most powerful communication vehicle of their generation.

Today's inexpensive digital camcorders and computers give students video-capturing and video-editing capabilities that were available only to professionals a few years ago. Technically, editing video using today's nonlinear editing systems available on low-end computers is simple and intuitive, yet it produces impressive results. Students feel empowered by their mastery of video and thoroughly enjoy having a new medium through which to communicate using images, music, narration, sound, text, and special effects.

Educationally, video production is a cross-curricular, collaborative experience that appeals to all types of learners and requires many different intelligences. By its nature, video production is cross curricular, combining writing, public speaking, acting, and aesthetic education with whatever subject matter your students are documenting. Video is produced in a collaborative environment, requiring students to be active, contributing, productive members of a video crew. Video production is sufficiently complicated and demanding to keep several students simultaneously involved, working in concert toward a common goal. Video production also appeals to many different types of learners and is made richer by the collaboration of students with varied intelligences. The students of a video crew must devote their various talents to the tasks of writing, storyboarding, directing, acting, capturing, editing, and distributing an idea on video. Your students will connect with the content material of their video on many different levels and in many different ways.

This book seeks to give you the confidence and resources to guide your students through the video production process. Section I focuses on the integration of video production into the classroom curriculum. Chapter 1 explains how video projects can enhance an existing curriculum and explores new educational opportunities afforded by the medium. It recommends ways to manage a cooperative learning environment, build evaluation rubrics for video projects, and assess student performance and learning objectives. Chapter 2 reviews the basic principles of the teaching of communication skills—such as message design and delivery, public speaking, acting, and nonverbal communication—for video productions. Chapter 3 is a primer on aesthetic education, covering the elements of communicating visually using video.

Section II breaks down the video production process into preproduction, production, and postproduction. Chapter 4 introduces preproduction, which involves the creation of a story through the text of a screenplay or script. The narrative is then given a visual dimension through storyboards. Chapter 5 explains how a professional video is produced, defines terminology, and offers helpful hints. Chapter 6 covers postproduction and nonlinear editors with a minimanual for iMovie and an overview of Pinnacle Studio version 7 and 8. In this chapter you will learn how to import the video into the computer from the camcorder as well as how to edit the video by cutting and sequencing and by adding text, music, voice-overs, transitions, and special effects. Chapter 7 discusses advanced nonlinear editing and DVD authoring tools that go beyond the basic capabilities of iMovie and Studio. Chapter 8 details the different distribution formats and compares the advantages and disadvantages of DVD, VHS, Video CD and CD ROMs. Section III helps you determine which video equipment is best suited for student productions. Chapter 9 discusses what to look for in a digital video camcorder and reviews four camcorders well suited for education. Chapter 10 acts as a buyer's guide, listing other equipment that is useful for video production and explaining which features are important.

Section IV, Chapter 11, discusses the important topic of media literacy in education today.

The appendix contains useful forms, student handouts, templates, and resources I have developed to facilitate the planning and implementation of digital video in the classroom.

A companion website, www.action-in-the-classroom.com, offers many useful resources and support material. All of the forms and worksheets in the book are available on this site in a variety of digital formats so that they can be downloaded, adjusted for your specific needs, and printed. Prepared presentations are also available to assist you in teaching the video production process and aesthetic elements, and every figure and table in the book is accessible on the web site. The user id and password for this website is *action*.

Taken together, this book and website cover all major aspects of video production and will serve as a guide and resource for you as you introduce video production into your curriculum and classroom. Video production is not to be undertaken lightly. It is demanding and will challenge you and your students in ways no other medium can. It can seem overwhelming and risky to lead a class into a project whose processes and technology are unfamiliar. However, your students will benefit from whatever exposure to video production they are afforded. Also, your students will profit from mistakes made, and the potential for continued improvement will motivate them with new and exciting opportunities. Your students will want to watch their video creations over and over again; they will be proud of their achievements and will always remember their first "professionally" produced video in your classroom.

So as they say in the video industry, "Quiet on the set. Standby talent. Roll tape. ACTION!"

Chapter One

Video Projects for the Classroom

Working with students and video is unusually rewarding and enriching. You and your students will truly enjoy the experience. My most memorable classroom projects are student-produced videos. Students are excited by video projects and immerse themselves in the experience and talk about them long after they are over.

Video projects require students to understand subject matter both on an emotional and intellectual level because video relates mood, tone, intensity, and feeling in addition to information. Your students, as video producers, must connect on all the levels to make a video that is as compelling as it is informative. After having worked with material so intimately, the students do not soon forget it.

Different video genres are available for different types of student projects. There are many to choose from to achieve your educational objectives. Each genre has educational potential, positive attributes, and specific demands. Choosing the right genre for each student project is crucial. Factors to consider when choosing a genre are curricular content, educational objectives, time and resource limitations, and the abilities of students.

The following is a brief description of the video genres and their educational potential. Each is explored in greater detail later in the chapter.

- Reality TV: A wildly popular newcomer to television, reality TV has educational potential as a training exercise to familiarize your students with the technical aspects of video production. Its appeal both educationally and commercially is that very little planning is necessary. Simply concoct a scenario, turn on a camera, and record. The results can be surprisingly good.

- Educational Video: An obvious choice for classroom use, educational video could be a demonstration or a report on a topic. A student could demonstrate how to solve a math problem or operate science lab equipment safely. A report could be prepared on any topic; but in either demonstration or report, the students become teachers without having to face their peers in a live performance.
- Documentary: The documentary is an excellent choice when serious study of a topic is desired. In this genre, students report on a topic with accuracy and honesty. Thorough research, in-depth understanding, careful planning, and clear writing are required for documentaries.
- News Report: The news report forces students to gather the answers to who, what, where, when, and why questions and report them in a succinct manner, complemented by visual images that support the information being related.
- Drama: By staging and videotaping a scene from a novel or reenacting a historical event, your students can better understand literature and history. A drama could also be used as a creative exercise, giving your students an opportunity to write, direct, and act in their own one-act play, for example.
- Foreign Film: The foreign film creates wonderful opportunities for students to practice their language skills in a taped performance; mistakes can be corrected by reshooting, and subsequent retakes reinforce the desired mastery.
- Commercial/Public Service Announcement (PSA): Commercials and PSAs are fun for the students to produce and will challenge them to condense a message that is entertaining and memorable into a 30-second spot. Having produced their own commercial or PSA, students become more sophisticated consumers in this market driven society.
- Music Video: Students will naturally gravitate to the music video, which will challenge them creatively. Music videos can be a useful way for students to practice music interpretation.
- Video Montage: A compilation of video imagery and sound, the video montage is a way for students to express themselves artistically through video.

For a video project to be valid, the students must know that their videos will have an audience. Tell them in advance who is going to see their work. Screening the videos in class is a minimum commitment. Other options include school assemblies, PTA meetings, parent nights, and public access TV. Some schools have film festivals or simply leave projects playing in a loop on a television in a common area of the school. The more people the students know will see their videos, the more effort they will put into their projects.

Let's take a closer look at each genre and explore the possibilities.

REALITY TV: A TRAINING EXERCISE

The video scavenger hunt is a highly entertaining activity that uses reality TV to teach the students how to work as a team, operate the camcorder, and manipulate the editing software. Almost no preproduction, or planning of the video, is required, and the results can be rewarding and very entertaining. This is the first activity I conduct in my videography class. It could also be used at the beginning of the year as an icebreaker activity that will acquaint the students with each other and the technical aspects of video production for future video-based projects.

The preproduction for this project is handed to the students in the form of a list of tasks with associated point values. Tasks can include activities as diverse as having team members act like a duck for 5 points per person, impersonate their favorite rock star for 50 points, serenade the principal or another teacher for 75 points, recite a poem publicly for 50 points—with a 50-point bonus if the students actually write the poem and people actually stop to listen. (A more complete list of possible tasks is listed in the appendix under "Video Scavenger Hunt Tasks.") Students are given a limited amount of time in which to videotape members of their team completing as many tasks as possible, competing for the highest point total. Then they are given a limited amount of time to import the video footage into a computer and edit it with titles, music, sound effects, and voiceovers. The results are frequently memorable.

I intentionally keep the job responsibilities loose by not assigning a director, camera operator, or editor, so that the students all get to try a little of everything. The project is not disadvantaged by this lack of specific crew assignments—as other projects might be—because it does not require the strict adherence to a director's vision, or consistency of talent and camera work, that most other productions require. All the students should be encouraged to try their hand at all aspects of the production that interest them. They will quickly find their niche in the group and be ready to volunteer their unique interests and talents in the next production.

A step-by-step guide for a video scavenger hunt:

1. Show camera operation and video aesthetic considerations to students using "Demonstration of Camcorder and Video Editing Software Lesson" (Available from the website).
2. Break the class up into groups of four or more students.
3. The day before the actual hunt, give the groups the list of tasks and their point values and time to discuss which tasks they are going to do. Ask them to bring in any props and/or music they might need or want for the hunt. Music they wish to add in the editing phase should be on a music CD.
4. On the day of the hunt, give a camcorder loaded with tape to the designated camera operator who is responsible for its care. Encourage everyone to try using the camera and to frame and light the picture correctly and record quality audio.
5. Send the students out to capture the tasks with a designated time to return. Points can be deduced for not returning on time.
6. After the time is up, teach the students how to import the video into a computer and edit their segments into a video. Have them start their video with a title shot that lists the members of their team on a black background, then another title shot identifying which task will be shown and its associated point value. Next, they should show the video of the task, followed by another title shot for the next task, and so on.
7. Encourage the students to add music, sound, and video effects as class time allows. These elements add greatly to the finished product.
8. Show the completed videos in class and possibly to the whole school. Your students will most certainly want to make copies for themselves.

Time allowed for this project should be brief because the purpose is not for the students to create a finished work but for them to learn to capture, edit, and export a video. I allow an hour and a half for video capture and two and a half hours for editing. Obviously you can adjust these times to comply with scheduling restraints.

The class then watches the videos together and totals the scores achieved by each video. The students will love the ease with which they can create a video that is funny and fast paced. Be sure to praise the students as they appear in the video. Discourage the mocking of individuals in a mean spirit, as students are already self-conscious enough, and this first experience with classroom video should be a positive one.

Do have the students pay close attention to the framing of the subjects, the quality of the audio and lighting, and the auto focus—zooming in and out—as it searches for its subject. Have them notice how the handheld camera shakes and how fast panning and zooming induce motion sickness in the audience. The students will invariably make many mistakes in all of these areas. This exercise is meant to allow them to make these mistakes and learn from them.

If time allows, it is useful to watch the entire video once through and then to go back and view each scene individually, having the team talk about what decisions they made and obstacles they had to overcome to capture and edit each scene. Have the team identify each shot as a long shot, medium close-up, close-up, or extreme close-up (chapter 3) and identify attributes such as a pan, tilt, zoom, or dolly (chapter 5). Also, have the team talk about the camera angle and perspective, lighting, audio, and sound and video effects choices they may have made and why (chapter 3).

To bring team members' attention to the aesthetic aspects of the video, you may want to award double the point value if they do a particularly good job of portraying an individual task through camera angles, effects, and/or music score.

If you choose to have your students do a video scavenger hunt, your students will enjoy the experience and be technically ready to tackle more challenging video projects.

EDUCATIONAL VIDEO: STUDENTS AS TEACHERS

The educational video gives students a chance to become teachers. We all know that the best way to truly understand a topic is to teach it to someone else. Unfortunately, this is a difficult task for a student to do, as it involves a live performance in front of a classroom of peers. Video allows students to teach without stage fright. It has the added advantage of allowing them to provide whatever props may be needed and to stage their presentation in the most effective location.

Educational videos can be used at any level and for any subject. They can demonstrate a process or explore a topic. The length and scope of the video can be as short as a minute and as simple as how to draw a circle, or as long and complex as a feature length report on World War II.

Students will often work much harder on a video project than they will on other assignments. As a typical example, I once assisted a pair of students who produced a video called "Hair Styles of the 20th Century" for a high school history class, as they had chosen to do a video project over the research paper option for this assignment. It turned out to be a well-researched piece that related hairstyles to the specific political and social events of their contemporary periods. They videotaped pictures of hairstyles and used voice-over for the names of the styles, relating them to the historic and political events of the time period in which they were fashionable. They even went so far as to style other classmates' hair and have them parade on a catwalk. In the end, the students admitted to having worked harder than normal on the project and felt they had learned a great deal. In this case, the teacher allowed the students to explore history using video, through a perspective that interested the students, making the subject of history much more personal and memorable.

The possibilities are endless. When choosing this genre, however, be careful to impress upon the students the importance of the content over visual effect. It should also be stressed that even though they are not writing a paper, proper use of grammar, format, vocabulary, and correct citation format are expected of them. The intent of this video genre is to teach. Special effects and music scores should complement the content matter, not distract from it. It is important to develop an assessment rubric to reinforce the relative value of each element of the video. More on assessment rubric development will appear later in this chapter.

DOCUMENTARY: STUDENTS
AS RECORDERS OF REALITY

Documentaries allow students to research and tell a story. This is the most challenging of the genres in that it requires depth of knowledge of the subject and the ability to represent that knowledge honestly and fairly on video. Research is an important part of this project. Interviews are frequently necessary, and the students need to be prepared with a list of questions and a firm understanding of the issues before the interview takes place so that no one's time is wasted.

Documentaries also allow the students to view a familiar subject from a new perspective. A group of high school students decided to create a documentary on the people behind the scenes at the school. It turned out to be a rewarding experience for everyone, since the students highlighted and learned about individuals who do not otherwise get much recognition. The individuals interviewed were honored to be recognized, and, as one of the video crew commented, "All we had to do was point a camera at them and ask them what they do, and they talked and talked. The problem was choosing what to take out."

Another group of high school students did a documentary on life in the junior kindergarten program at their school. This assignment involved the crew's becoming familiar with the daily routine and educational objectives of the junior kindergarten and shooting a couple of hours of video from a low angle to simulate the vantage point of a four-year-old. High school students representing the school from the perspective of a junior kindergartener turned out to be enlightening and enjoyable and taught them a lesson in the power of perspective.

NEWS REPORT: STUDENTS AS REPORTERS

The news report has obvious applications in an English or journalism class. News reports can be especially useful for announcements if your school has a closed-circuit cable network allowing broadcasts to be sent directly into homerooms. However, a cable network is certainly not necessary to deliver news reports. School assembly viewings are another delivery strategy and venue for showing news reports. The possibilities for newscasts range from creating a single newsreel to a sustained broadcast of daily announcements. Your schedule and time allotted to this project will dictate the sophistication of the production(s).

An important aspect of this genre is public speaking. Here students see the practical importance of proper posture, pronunciation, punctuation, articulation, sincerity, rhythm, pace, and vocal variety. Public speaking skills are covered in more detail in chapter 2.

Another important aspect of this genre is the use of "establishing shots" and "B-roll" footage. An establishing shot is the opening scene of a story that contextualizes the newscast. For instance, a shot of a soccer or field hockey game before a report about a proposed athletic field provides a visual cue about the topic. The shot visually clues the viewer in to the topic of the news report. B-roll video is the footage that supports the newscast; it is interspersed in the A-roll footage of an anchorperson or interviewer. An example is the cutaway shot to students walking in the halls and checking their lockers while the voice of an anchorperson continues to report on education in America. Establishing shots and B-roll footage are explored further in chapter 5.

DRAMA: STUDENTS AS WRITERS AND ACTORS

Drama, as a type of video, allows students to connect with literature or history through the staging of a scene from a novel or reenactment of a historic event. A drama can also be used as a creative exercise, giving students an opportunity to write, direct, and act in their own screenplay.

The junior kindergarten students at my school act in their own dramas and have them recorded on videotape. With the help of their teacher, a designated student creates a storyline, the teacher or aide taking dictation. The student then chooses classmates to be fellow actors and directs their efforts. When the stage is set, the teacher narrates the story, the students act, and a teacher's aide records the story on videotape. The students will want to watch these videos over and over and share them with their parents. The teacher also retains a copy as part of the students' portfolios.

At higher grade levels, students can be assigned to bring to life their favorite scenes from literature. There is no better way to have students experience the emotion or complexity of a story then to ask them to reenact a scene or excerpt from the book. It forces them to become the characters and walk in their shoes. The students will have to know more than just what the characters did; they will have to understand the characters' motivation, state of mind, relationship to other characters, social status, morality, and then mimic the characters' personality. Acting is a powerful way to interact with a text, and video facilitates the capture and delivery of such performances.

FOREIGN FILM: STUDENTS AS FOREIGN SPEAKERS

The foreign language department in my school has been a leader in making videos; for years our French department teachers have been requiring students to script, rehearse, and produce a video in French. The topics vary from year to year, but this year the students in French IV were required to make a video tour of the school. The French teacher observes that some students who are quiet and nonparticipatory in class choose to take leading roles in a video.

COMMERCIAL: STUDENTS AS SALESPEOPLE

The commercial is entertaining for students to produce and will challenge them to condense a message that is engaging and memorable into a 30-second spot. While this genre of video does not take as long as others, students will be surprised at how difficult it is to communicate effectively in such a short period of time. I find that one and a half minutes is a more reasonable amount of time to give students attempting to shoot a commercial for the first time.

The subjects of students' commercials can be fictitious products. Students can be creative and market a watch that can take you back in time ten seconds to correct a mistake, or smart pills to increase academic ability. Or commercials can be informative and educational; have students sell conjunctions or semicolons to improve writing, or market the quadratic equation to solve difficult math problems (Limpus 1994, 43).

Your students should try to create a marketing strategy for the product that will construct an association between the product they are promoting and something desirable, as is done in the advertising industry. The "Got Milk?" campaign associates glamorous and famous figures with drinking milk, signified by the milk mustaches they all wear. Pepsi appeals to young people, "The Next Generation," claiming Pepsi is "what it takes to be young." These campaigns try to associate a liquid from a cow and a carbonated soft drink with glamour and youth.

As a homework assignment before they produce their own commercial, have the students watch for, list, and then analyze their favorite commercials. Have them pay special attention to associations the marketers are trying to create in hopes of promoting their product as a necessary ingredient to being socially acceptable, physically attractive, and all other things desirable. Also have students watch for "expert testimony" and quasi-scientific demonstrations. By producing their own commercial and attempting to create their own advertising campaigns, students become more keenly aware of the techniques used in marketing and become more sophisticated and discerning consumers.

PUBLIC SERVICE ANNOUNCEMENTS (PSAs): STUDENTS AS PUBLIC SERVANTS

Having students produce public service announcements is a way to connect them to health related education like antidrug and antismoking education. Here they have the opportunity to craft their own message about public health issues. This is not a new concept in the health curriculum, but it gives the students another avenue of expression.

Public service announcements do not have to be an anti-campaign, they could also be created to inform the public about the importance of fire detectors, the hazards of playing with matches, the dangers of playing with household chemicals, and so on.

MUSIC VIDEO: STUDENTS AS ROCK STARS

Producing a music video has great potential for music classes. Video offers the exciting mixture of visual and auditory stimulation, a combination that has profoundly changed the popular music industry.

Our students have never known a time when their popular music has not been made into videos. The average preteen or teenager is very familiar with, and is a great fan of, music videos. Even preschool children are inundated with music videos on such stations as the Disney Channel and

Cartoon Network, as well as in places like Chuck-e-Cheese. Much has been made of children who have been robbed of the enjoyment that comes from creating their own mental interpretations of the music because they are exposed to video images for all of their favorite songs. Here is an opportunity for them to create and share their own interpretation of a musical work on video.

Students will jump at the opportunity to create their own music video. You can let them choose the song or assign them a piece you want them to interpret. Be sure to acquaint them with the three basic approaches to music video production: the performance video, in which the students dress up like the singers and create a concertlike performance; the pantomimed story, in which the students act out a story suggested by the music; and the montage of images, a surreal conglomeration of images suggested by the music. Most videos contain all three elements (Limpus 1994, 65).

VIDEO MONTAGE: STUDENTS AS ARTISTS

The video montage, sometimes called experimental or artistic video, allows your students to explore new ways of using the medium. While a video montage could be part of another video, such as a music video, it could also stand alone as an aesthetic entity with the interpretation left to the viewer. This genre is useful for any art or photography class that teaches imagery and aesthetics. Students can be set free to create videos that contain only images and sounds with no narration, yet elicit strong emotional responses.

Video is a recognized art form and occasionally you will see art museums mount exhibits of abstract experimental videos. Some of your students, however, will enjoy creating their own video abstractions; they may become future video artists whose shows will tour art museums around the country.

Two students once made a video montage that paralleled the poem *The Love Song of J. Alfred Prufrock* by T. S. Eliot as an English assignment. They used music inspired by the poem and tried hard to recreate the visual images that the poem inspires. Admittedly, it was very difficult to follow if you were not intimately familiar with the poem, but it was produced exclusively for the English classes that were reading the poem. The students and teachers were very impressed with the ability of these students to give this poem a visual existence and match the mood and content, while using contemporary music that was inspired by a poem written in 1919.

It is not too early for students to think about their work being displayed publicly. There are many venues for amateur film productions. Todd Pankoff, a professional video producer, once advised my students on a tour of his studio that if they want to work with video as a career, there is no better time to start then now. He notes that video making is not a field restricted to those with an advanced education in video production. He advises students who are interested in making video to begin to work with the medium as soon as possible. While advanced instruction will certainly help them learn the finer points, there is a great deal they can learn through untrained experience and experimentation.

VIDEO PRODUCTION IN A COOPERATIVE
LEARNING ENVIRONMENT

Video requires a team effort. There are simply too many variables and tasks simultaneously needing attention for one person to do justice to them all. Most productions need students to act as screenwriters, camera operators, costume and set designers, talent (actors), directors, technical directors, and editors. It is in this collaborative environment that diverse student talents can be celebrated and disparate personalities constructively employed. In video production, there is a role for everyone. A complete list of positions and responsibilities appears in chapter 5.

Your role in all video productions in your classroom is that of producer. The producer is a "suit" (term for businessperson in video industry) and is responsible for seeing that a video is created on time and on budget. You are responsible for hiring a crew (your students) to make the video you request. You will want to hire a good crew to produce your video, making sure that each member of the crew is appropriately matched to the responsibility.

When preparing your students for their first video project, explain all the crew positions and responsibilities and have your students think about what strengths they might bring to the production. Then have them decide on the positions in which they would feel comfortable. Or you might want to assign positions and rotate students through different positions during the production to make sure everyone gets some time in each one.

The creative students will be attracted to the position of screenwriter, the person responsible for creating the story or content of the video. This person not only writes the script but also mocks up the initial visuals for the video in storyboards (more on storyboards in chapter 4). Frequently, much of the storyline and many other ideas for a project will come from brainstorming sessions with the entire video crew. It then becomes the screenwriter's responsibility to consolidate these ideas in a coherent script with storyboards.

The more active, outgoing students will gravitate toward the role of talent, which involves being in front of the camera as actors. Their high energy and exuberance will be an asset to the final product. The inevitable gigglefest will break out during their initial video shoot, which will test your patience and resolve. It will end as the novelty wears off and the embarrassment fades away.

The leaders in your class will be attracted to the role of director. The person chosen for this position will have the vision of what the final product will look like. This person will also have to be confident enough to direct the efforts of his or her peers and make sure the crew stays on task. The director is the leader and has the final word on any differences of opinion the group may have during production. It is a difficult and important responsibility.

Generally, the introverted students will want the behind-the-scenes positions such as camera operator. This position requires an artistic eye. The camera operator must be able to see the image in the viewfinder as a whole picture, one that requires composition and framing. This person's job is made more difficult by the fact that the subjects in the viewfinder are moving, and the camera requires constant adjustment just to keep them in the picture, in focus, and part of a composition. This is a mentally and physically tiring job, as camera operators are constantly thinking about the composition of the picture, trying to anticipate the movements of subjects, and twisting and turning the camera and their bodies to get the right shot. After each shot, camera operators will find themselves needing a deep breath.

Other attractive positions for behind-the-scenes staff are editor and technical director. The editor is responsible for taking the raw footage and piecing it together to make a finished product. A technical director is responsible for moving the raw footage into a finished product, but does so under the direction of the editor. Frequently in student productions, the editor will act as his or her own technical director. However, the position of technical director is well suited for a student who is good with computers. The editor and technical director positions require patience and attention to detail. Facility with technical equipment and the proper temperament for working with computers and hardware are a bonus in this position.

Other behind-the-scenes positions include costume, makeup, set, and props staff. These people conceive and create the visual effects that can add greatly to any production. When someone is assigned to these positions, more attention is given to these details.

You can see there is something for everyone in video production. I suggest groups of four or more per video crew. There is plenty to do to keep four students continuously engaged. As in the real film and video industry, one individual may fill more than one role and some crews may have more than one actor or screenwriter.

ASSIGNING STUDENTS TO A POSITION (CASTING THE CREW)

Defining each person's position in the crew is an important step in video production. Without it, a group is prone either to founder, as all members try to influence the production in keeping with their individual visions, or stall, because everyone is hesitant to fill necessary roles. Production is difficult at best when too many people are involved in the editing or directing of a video.

Once the class is familiar with the roles and responsibilities of the crew members, you can allow a self-selection process to take place or assign the students to roles. If you allow the students to self-select, have them choose a position and then you create crews by assigning a camera operator, director, editor, talent, and whatever other positions are necessary to each group. Obviously, one person can fill more than one role, and most positions other than director can accommodate more than one person.

The most important position to define is that of director, giving each crew a leader who can act as arbiter and ultimate decision maker. In the video industry, the director is the parent figure of the group, frequently being the most experienced member of the crew and commanding their collective respect. It is important that the director be responsible and

Student Video Project Proposal

Name(s): _____

Title: _____

Purpose: _____

_____

Audience: _____

Genre:
- ❑ Educational
- ❑ Documentary
- ❑ News Broadcast
- ❑ Kids Video
- ❑ Commercial
- ❑ Game Show
- ❑ Foreign Film
- ❑ Drama
- ❑ Action
- ❑ Reality TV
- ❑ Comedy
- ❑ Music Video
- ❑ Video Montage

Elements:
- ❑ Interviews
- ❑ Live Action
- ❑ Staged Performance
- ❑ Narration
- ❑ Music
- ❑ Special Effects
- ❑ Titles/Subtitles
- ❑ Graphics
- ❑ Pixilation
- ❑ VR
- ❑ Video of Pictures
- ❑ Imported Video

Equipment Needed:
- ❑ DV Camcorder
- ❑ DV Tape(s)
- ❑ Tripod
- ❑ Handheld Mic
- ❑ Lavaliere Mic
- ❑ Boom Mic
- ❑ DV Editing Comp
- ❑ External HD
- ❑ TV/VCR
- ❑ Lights
- ❑ Reflector
- ❑ Dolly
- ❑ Clapstick/Slate

❑ Costumes: _____

❑ Sets: _____

❑ Props: _____

Locations: _____

_____

Schedule:
Project due on: _____   Preproduction completed by: _____

Production completed by: _____   Postproduction completed by: _____

Distribution Format:
- ❑ DVD
- ❑ MiniDV
- ❑ VHS
- ❑ Digital 8
- ❑ Video CD
- ❑ Hi8
- ❑ CD ROM
- ❑ Web

Archiving: Archive up to 4.7 GB of computer files on Data DVD disk for future edits? ❑ Yes ❑ No

Crew:
Producer/Director: _____

Scriptwriter: _____

Camera Operator: _____

Talent: _____

Editor: _____

APPROVED BY: _____   Date: _____

Figure 1.1   Student Video Project Proposal Form

fair, for this person must make sure that everyone is heard, their opinions valued—and their disputes resolved.

The director should report back to you frequently so that you can track the crew's progress and the director's management of the project. Before the crew starts shooting the video, make sure that the director has a vision and realistic plan. Have the director "pitch" you the idea as if he or she were trying to sell you the concept and execution of a production. Make sure the group completes a Student Video Project Proposal (figure 1.1). Establish that your approval is required before they begin production and impress upon them that 80 percent of the work for a video is completed before the cameras are even loaded. If the vision and plan are clearly defined, the production of the video will go more smoothly. If the vision is not defined, the crew will have trouble deciding what to shoot or how to edit the video. Throughout the project, be sure to help the directors juggle the many interests, visions, and personalities of their crews.

ASSESSMENT RUBRICS FOR VIDEO PROJECTS

To ensure that video projects are meeting educational objectives, it is important to create an assessment rubric—a checklist of required and desirable elements and their relative value to the completed project. Rubrics are useful for all project-based educational assessment. Creating a rubric helps you plan, ensure the educational merit of, and assess the video projects. Rubrics give the students a starting point and framework on which to build their project with confidence, as the rubrics communicate what elements are required and which you consider to be most important. A sample rubric is displayed in figure 1.2.

In video, the three main elements of assessment are content, communication, and presentation. Content is the information conveyed within the video. Communication is the means by which that content is conveyed. Presentation is how the project looks and sounds: the quality of picture and audio, effective use of music, choice of camera angles, costumes, and special effects.

Frequently, students become preoccupied with presentation when first working with video. They think of funny scenarios or envision scenes for the project and want to jump right in and start shooting footage to recreate these scenes for their video.

Assessment Rubric for Video Project

Project:_____

Students:_____

Content—60 points (60%)

Mastery of material:
Identified important points of topic (15)_____
Correctly stated the facts (15)_____
Explained using good language skills (10)_____

Research:
Encyclopedia resource (4)____
3 print materials resource (4)____
2 online resources (4)____
Conducted 2 interviews (4)____

Bibliography:
    Correct citation (4) _____
Comments:

Content:_____

Communication & Presentation—40 points (40%)

Communication Strategy:
❑ Narration (5)____
❑ Interview (5)____
❑ Still Images (5)____
❑ Music (5)____
❑ Text/Graphics (5)____

Presentation:
Video Quality (5)____
Sound Quality (5)____
Use of Camera Angles (3)____
Appropriate Transitions (1)____
Opening Title/Closing Credits w/Bib. (1)____

Comments:

Communication & Presentation:_____

Extra Credit—5 points

Effective use of:
❑ Special Video Effects ❑ Special Audio Effects ❑ Costuming/Dress/Props
❑ Animation/Pixilation ❑ Imported Video ❑ Symbolism
❑ Virtual Reality ❑ Live Action ❑ Staged Performance
❑ Other:

Extra Credit:_____

Overall Comments:

Total Points:_____
Letter Grade:_____

Figure 1.2   Sample Assessment Rubric for Video Projects

The difficulty for you as the teacher is to get the students to concentrate on the content of the video. Researching the topic should be required before any shooting and editing takes place. The students must know a great deal about their topic before they even think about putting together a video. It is important that they understand the topic both intellectually and emotionally so that they create a video that not only conveys facts but appropriately expresses mood.

After the students have researched their topic and have a good grasp of the material, they will need to think about how they want to communicate their topic through video. There are many possibilities to choose from:

- act as a reporter or anchor—be a talking head
- conduct interviews, shoot footage of live action (such as a sporting event or protest)
- stage a performance
- narrate the video with a voice-over
- import or shoot video of still images
- capture video from another video source (such as movies or TV)
- create computer animations or pixilation (a sequence of still pictures that when played together animate an object)
- render graphics, type text, use computer to generate virtual reality
- employ video and sound special effects, and use a soundtrack.

You may want to require elements for each project or give the students a list of possible options and have them employ three or more appropriate to the project.

Spend some time going over the assessment rubric with the students to identify what the projects must contain and which aspects of their projects have higher point values and therefore should receive more attention. In the sample (figure 1.2), the total possible points are listed in parentheses with a line to record the earned points for each aspect. Each section is subtotaled, with a grand total at the end. You can adjust values, add and subtract categories and elements to create the assessment rubric that fits your curriculum and assessment needs.

In the sample rubric (figure 1.2) content is weighted the most, stressing the importance of that component. Content includes mastery of the material (40 percent) and research and bibliography (20 percent). When working with curriculum material, it is important that the students are able to identify important points, correctly state facts, and cover the topic in sufficient detail, as well as account for their research methods and resources. As content is 60 percent of the total grade, students will see the need to spend a significant amount of time researching and understanding their topics before they even consider production. For this reason, video projects are useful as cumulative assignments in which all the information the students have learned in a unit can come together.

The communication and presentation section, while not as heavily weighted as the content section, still contains crucial aspects. In communication strategy (25 percent) you will evaluate the effectiveness of the various required elements. In the example, students are required to narrate their video with appropriate facts, conduct an interview, show video footage of still images, render text and graphics, and lay a music soundtrack somewhere in their video. As you are watching the video, check off the required elements using the boxes to the left. At the end, rate the effective use of each element.

The presentation section (15 percent), as mentioned before, will be the focus for some students. For the most part, presentation items are the technical aspects of the video dealing with quality of picture and sound. However, while quality sound and video are critically important in commercial video, with transition shots adding to visual excitement, they should not be given undue weight in educational uses of video. It is unnecessary to encourage students to refine their presentation by giving it a high point value. Students will labor to perfect sound and video quality regardless, as a matter of personal interest and enjoyment.

You may decide to award extra credit for other elements included on the rubric but not required. Sometimes these pleasantly surprising elements are quite effective and extra credit is, of course, your choice.

A narrative response in the comments line allows you to react to each section individually and to the project as a whole. Here you have the opportunity to explain your awarding of points, praise students' knowledge of the material or use of video techniques, make recommendations, or comment on their video as a whole.

A point total is calculated at the bottom of the rubric and a final letter grade is assigned (if you use letter grades). The assessment rubric does not eliminate the subjective nature of grading, since you will still have to make judgments as to how many points to award, but it does establish requirements and priorities and takes some of the mystery out of the grading procedure for the students.

Chapter Two

Communication Skills
in Video Production

Video as a medium of communication involves message design, script writing, acting, public speaking, music, sound effects, costumes, and props. This chapter explores each specific aspect of video production.

MESSAGE DESIGN

When planning to produce a video, students must understand that they are creating a message with a purpose and target audience. In order to make the message effective, students should ask themselves, "What is the purpose of this video?" All aspects of the video should advance this purpose. The students should also ask a closely related question, "What do I hope to achieve?" Stating the purpose and goal up front will clarify direction and give the students a yardstick by which to measure the components of their video.

The students will then need to identify the target audience of the message. Who are they trying to reach? Demographics of the intended viewers should be detailed: age, ethnicity, education, occupation, socioeconomic status, geography, politics, religious beliefs, and so on. Once the target audience is identified, the students should research this group's interests, issues, language, culture, icons, music, and fashions. The students should then employ images, argot, and information that will reach and "speak to" this audience in their video.

The two questions of purpose and audience are included in the Student Video Project Proposal (figure 2.1), which students should be required to complete and have approved before any videotaping takes

Student Video Project Proposal

Name(s): George L., Beth G., Sahale G., Chris B., Abby W.

Title: The Battle at Gettysburg - A Special Report

Purpose: To inform viewers of the events at the Battle of Gettysburg in a CNN like format

Audience: People of 1863 who would have been interested in knowing

Genre:
- ❏ Educational
- ❏ Documentary
- ☒ News Broadcast
- ❏ Kids Video
- ❏ Commercial
- ❏ Game Show
- ❏ Foreign Film
- ❏ Drama
- ❏ Action
- ❏ Reality TV
- ❏ Comedy
- ❏ Music Video
- ❏ Video Montage

Elements:
- ☒ Interviews
- ❏ Live Action
- ☒ Staged Performance
- ❏ Narration
- ❏ Music
- ❏ Special Effects
- ☒ Titles/Subtitles
- ☒ Graphics (maybe)
- ❏ Pixilation
- ❏ VR
- ☒ Video of Pictures
- ❏ Imported Video

Equipment Needed:
- ☒ DV Camcorder
- ☒ DV Tape(s)
- ☒ Tripod
- ☒ Handheld Mic
- ☒ Lavaliere Mic
- ❏ Boom Mic
- ❏ DV Editing Comp
- ❏ External HD
- ❏ TV/VCR
- ☒ Lights
- ☒ Reflector
- ❏ Dolly
- ☒ Clapstick/Slate

☒ Costumes: Anchors - Suites, Reporter - Casual, Soldier - Union uniform

❏ Sets: _____

☒ Props: Musket

Locations: Beth's back yard, Lunchroom table (News Studio)

Schedule:

Project due on: 10/25   Preproduction completed by: 10/13

Production completed by: 10/18   Postproduction completed by: 10/23

Distribution Format: ☒ DVD   ☒ VHS   ❏ Video CD   ❏ CD ROM   ❏ Web
         ❏ MiniDV   ❏ Digital 8   ❏ Hi8

Archiving: Archive up to 4.7 GB of computer files on Data DVD disk for future edits? ❏ Yes ❏ No

Crew:

Producer/Director: Sahale

Scriptwriter: George, Chris

Camera Operator: Chris

Talent: Abby - Anchor, Beth - Reporter, George - Soldier

Editor: Abby, Beth

APPROVED BY: _____ Date: 10/9

Figure 2.1   **Student Video Project Proposal Form**

place. The logistics of student proposals and preproduction planning are discussed further in chapter 4.

Other questions for students to ask are: "Why is the audience watching this?" and "Is it a captive audience or a self-selecting group of interested viewers?" Captive viewers will require convincing that the video is relevant to their interests or needs. The interest of the self-selecting group can be taken for granted. "How much do the viewers know about the subject?" The video should not speak down to, or over the head of, its audience. "What do they expect?" It is risky to surprise an audience and deviate widely from expectations.

Answering these questions will help students design a targeted message that will reach the intended audience and achieve the anticipated response. Message design is an art for which there is no better teacher than experience.

TREATMENT AND OUTLINE OF VIDEO PROJECTS

After the students have established their purpose and analyzed their target audience, they will have to draft the treatment. *Treatment* is a term used for the written outline, in general terms, of the storyline, characters, informational content, location of scenes, and dominant images in the video. The treatment, known as a design concept in the theatre, must also adopt one of three production styles: presentational, in which the actor speaks to the audience; realistic, in which the actors perform as though they are unaware of the camera and audience; and expressionistic, in which images and sounds are used in highly symbolic and expressive ways.

Here is a sample student project treatment for a presentational production about the Battle of Gettysburg for a group of five students, Abby, Tom, Lisa, Matt, and Chris:

Abby and Tom act as anchorpersons on a CNN-type news broadcast of the Battle of Gettysburg. Tom and Abby open the news broadcast with a special report about the battle. Abby lists the generals and their armies and describes basic troop movements; she is aided by hand-drawn maps. Tom lists the casualties and describes the conditions under which the fighting is taking place. The coanchors go to a reporter at the scene, Lisa, who interviews Matt, a Confederate soldier, about his experience in the battle. Lisa next turns to Chris, a Union soldier, and interviews him. When the interviews conclude, we return to Abby and Tom in the studio. A newsflash is handed to Tom and Abby by the cameraman; it declares that the Confederate forces at Gettysburg have surrendered, making the Union armies victorious. Tom and Abby announce the details of the surrender. They promise to keep the audience informed of future developments as the station is about to take a short commercial break. The broadcast fades to black, which is the end of the production.

A sample realistic treatment using the same group of students and topic follows:

Lisa and Abby are nurses in a M.A.S.H.-type first aid tent on the edge of the Battle of Gettysburg. Abby is training the new nurse, Lisa, on how to care for the wounded. Abby talks to Lisa about the types of injuries inflicted during the Civil War and their contemporary treatments. Matt, Tom, and Chris are acting as the wounded. They are lying on the ground inside the tent and are relating personal experiences of the battle to one another. The camera switches back and forth between Lisa and Abby tending to the wounded and Matt, Tom, and Chris talking about the battle. The scene ends with Abby deciding to go get the doctor because she believes that Tom's leg must be amputated. Tom puts up a fight but Abby and Lisa anesthetize him. As Tom loses consciousness, the picture fades to black, which ends the production.

A sample expressionistic treatment for the same group and topic could be a montage of the Gettysburg Address, as follows:

The video opens on a black screen with a mournful bugle slowly playing taps. The picture slowly fades in to a picture of Gettysburg. As bugle plays on, other pictures of Gettysburg fade in and out, matching the tempo of the music. The music fades and a still image of Lincoln appears while all five members of the cast read together the opening paragraph of the Gettysburg Address. Tom reads the first sentence in the second paragraph, and the picture fades into battle scenes. Abby reads the next two sentences, and other members rotate reading lines alone as pictures change to reflect the words of the speech. In the last sentence, beginning with "that this nation, under God," all five students read together the concluding words as a picture of the Lincoln Memorial appears. After the Address is completed, the last stanza of taps is played and the picture fades to black. (figure 2.2)

After the treatment has been established, the group will need to outline some of the details of the production: what information has to be gathered, what locations will be used, what the schedule is, and who is responsible for what. Again, each production's outline will look different; a commercial's outline would be short compared to a lengthy outline for a documentary.

After establishing the treatment and outline, the students should meet with you to pitch their proposal. Here the students should explain the purpose of their video, its target audience, and their strategy for reaching this audience. Next they should pitch their treatment and outline for their production. You will then guide them, helping them shape a project that is acceptable and possible, given the limitations of time and resources. As most of the videos produced in your classroom will lack any funding or transportation to remote locations, students' options will be somewhat limited. But I am always amazed at what is possible with a little creativity and ingenuity. Your ability to judge a project's feasibility and help your students improvise with no budget and little time will improve with experience.

Depending on the ability of your students and the time allowed for projects, you may need to omit the requirement that students come up with their own treatments and assign pre-scripted treatments to crews as a starting point for their productions. This can save time while allowing students to fill in the outlines creatively, research the topics, and write complete scripts for their productions.

SCRIPTWRITING

After the treatment has been established and an outline written, a script will need to be written to describe in detail the visual and auditory elements of the video. Scripts vary from one video genre to another. A script for a talk show may consist of only a list of guests and possible questions, while a script for a one-act play will contain every word spoken and all camera and talent direction.

There are two types of scripts, single and double column. The single-column script mixes the directions for camera and talent with the text in paragraph form on a page. I have my students use the two-column script format exclusively (figure 2.2). Here students list the visual and camera directions in the left column and audio and textual information on the

Visual and Camera Directions	Audio and Narration Directions
Black	Bugle playing taps slowly (taps.mp3)
Fade in to picture of Gettysburg • Gettysburg1.jpg	
Pan pictures of Gettysburg • Page 21 of book 1 • Page 45 of book 1	
Fade to black	Taps fades to silence
Fade in to picture of Lincoln standing • Page 15 of book 3	**All read:** Four score and seven years ago our fathers brought forth upon this continent, a new nation, conceived in liberty, and dedicated to the proposition that all men are created equal.
Fade to panning pictures of battle scenes • Page 102 of book 1	**Tom:** Now we are engaged in a great civil war, testing whether that nation, or any nation so conceived and so dedicated, can long endure.
Continue with battle scenes • Page 56 of book 3 • Page 57 of book 3 • Page 67 of book 3	**Abby:** We are met on a great battlefield of that war. We have come to dedicate a portion of that field, as a final resting place for those who here gave their lives that this nation might live. It is altogether fitting and proper that we should do this.
Begin scenes with wounded and dead • Page 224 of book 1 • Page 312 of book 2	**Chris:** But in a larger sense, we cannot dedicate—we cannot consecrate—we cannot hallow—this ground. The brave men, living and dead, who struggled here, have consecrated it, far above our poor power to add or detract.
Begin pictures of group photos of soldiers • Page 24 of book 2 • Page 14 of book 3	**Lisa:** The world will little note, nor long remember what we say here, but it can never forget what they did here. It is for us, the living, rather to be dedicated here to the unfinished work which they who fought here have thus far so nobly advanced.
Begin pictures of reconstruction • Page 225 of book 4 • Page 315 of book 3	**Matt:** It is rather for us to be here dedicated to the great task remaining before us, that from these honored dead we take increased devotion to that cause for which they gave the last full measure of devotion; that we here highly resolve that these dead shall not have died in vain;
Fade to picture of Lincoln Memorial • Lincoln.jpg	**All:** that this nation, under God, shall have a new birth of freedom, and that this government of the people, by the people, and for the people shall not perish from this earth.
	Fade in last stanza of taps from bugle (taps.mp3)
Fade to black	Fade to silence

Figure 2.2 Two Column Script Example: Gettysburg Address Video Montage Script

right. This side-by-side breakdown helps the students organize the visual and audio content of the video.

STORYBOARDS

A more visual description of the proposed video can be depicted through storyboards (figure 2.3). In storyboarding, students draw an actual picture of what shots will look like in a viewfinder-shaped box. The storyboards are sequenced and titled, camera and talent directions are given, and the text and audio portions are written below. For visually intensive productions, the students will find the storyboards more helpful than a script. On the storyboards, students will be composing shots: deciding on camera angles, subjects, perspectives, locations, props, and costumes. I demonstrate storyboards by using stick figure drawings so that those students who, like me, lack artistic ability are not intimidated when creating their own storyboards. Software is also available to help students create professional-looking storyboards with drag and drop icons and scenic backdrops. Further description of storyboards is available in chapter 4.

Figure 2.3   Storyboard Template

PUBLIC SPEAKING AND VIDEO

Teachers of public speaking have been using video successfully for years to record and evaluate student performances. As in all performance-based education, having the students evaluate themselves is crucial to their improvement. Videotaped recordings of their public speeches allow the students to witness their performance as a spectator, assessing their volume, articulation, pronunciation, voice quality, vocal variety, energy, rhythm and pace, punctuation, breath support, sincerity, use of sentence interrupters (such as *uhm*), body movements, and eye contact.

In almost all video productions, students will be required to perform some sort of public speaking, in their roles as anchorpersons, reporters, actors, or narrators. Their stage presence and quality of narration can be greatly enhanced by their knowing and adhering to the basic principles of public speaking.

Some of these skills take on special significance in video, where it is imperative that the talent use good elocution to make themselves understood. This is especially true on videotape, where audio fidelity can be compromised by the quality and placement of equipment, poor acoustics, and distracting ambient sounds on location. Often the most difficult aspect of video production is recording clear audio. Poor audio is the most frequent detractor in student-produced videos. Technical aspects of recording good audio will be discussed in chapter 5, but even more important than recording techniques is the quality of the talents' original presentation. Editors in postproduction will not be able to compensate technically for inaudible or unclear speech.

Beyond concerns of simply being heard, vocal variety adds to the interest of the listener; by animating the voice, the speaker has a better chance of attracting and keeping the viewer's attention. Students can animate their voices by using inflection when asking a question, whispering to denote a secret, yelling for exclamation, or just changing pitch. The speaker's voice should convey the appropriate emotions of sincerity, excitement, resentment, anger, and jealousy. The voice tempo, loudness, pitch, and inflection should match the emotion of the message; otherwise the students risk having the audience disregard their presentation as insincere. Such simple effects can go a long way in adding to the quality of a presentation. Listeners will appreciate the vocal variety and reward the video with their attention.

The rhythm and pacing of public speaking is generally slower than the pacing of normal conversation. Heavily coached public speakers will speak almost half as fast as they would in normal conversation (Cook 1989, 168). It is also important for the speaker to find a rhythm and tempo that match the mood of the content. Cuts between shots, fades, and the motion of the video should match the tempo of the narration. For example, if the narrator is talking quickly, the images should also flash by quickly.

Pauses in presentation are very important in public speaking, and even more so in video narration; the "pause for effect" is useful for giving the audience time to process what has been said. Silence also focuses the viewer's attention on the video image, which sometimes can convey a message or emotion most effectively. It is also useful to pause the narration if the audience is expected to assimilate a complicated visual, such as a chart or written text. Students should try to avoid oversaturating the audience with visual and auditory information. A long pause in audio can also be used to signify a transition from one concept to another. Silence or a break in narration is more easily inserted in a video presentation, since the presenter does not feel the audience staring at him or her during the silence.

The physical movements of a speaker are most easily evaluated on video. Students in a public speaking role frequently concentrate on their text and ignore their body movements. Watching videotaped performances of themselves speaking is the best way for students to become aware of their movements and modify their behavior. A useful exercise in checking for repetitive and distractive body movements on videotape is to mute the sound and fast-forward through the taped performance; distracting and repetitive behavior will become exaggerated and apparent.

Breath support becomes noticeable when the speaker is having trouble getting enough air in and out to finish a sentence or produce a loud enough voice. Nervousness will compromise breathing and the ability to sustain a satisfactory voice. Students need to relax and take a deep breath before they speak. An advantage of video production is that it allows nervous presenters multiple retakes, giving them the time and repetition necessary to relax and control their breathing. However, a formal education in public speaking would not be complete without students' learning how to present under pressure, in front of people, in a live performance.

DIFFERENCES BETWEEN VIDEO
PRODUCTION AND PUBLIC SPEAKING

Video productions beg for more visual stimulation than is usually available in a live public speech. Video audiences are accustomed to a steady stream of visual stimulation beyond the talking head. In fact, our students demand all types of stimulation to maintain their attention, as they have been raised in a culture where overstimulation is the norm. And video does like movement. When showing still images on video, it is a good idea to pan over the pictures or fade them in and out. However, this obsession with motion can be taken to the extreme, as is popular today on kids' shows where even stationary talking heads move around the screen as the camera zooms in and out and rocks back and forth off angle, adding movement to what is otherwise a stationary image. I find this camera technique annoying and distracting, but it is a legitimate technique the students are frequently exposed to, and, as a result, you might see some of it in your students' productions. The tolerance for this technique seems to be determined by generation, as my students and children do not seem bothered at all by the "moving" talking head.

Videotaped messages also lack the real-time audience feedback a public speaker enjoys while giving a presentation. Hence, the creator of a video message is not able to adjust the message based on the audience's real-time reactions. To rectify this lack of audience feedback, the video industry sometimes produces shows in front of a live studio audience, giving the actors a chance to play to the audience's reactions.

Student productions will not normally have the advantage of a studio audience. You should encourage your students to perform and imagine the audience's reaction. The speakers should always envision that the audience is "with" them and that their reactions are positive.

ACTING

Acting will often be required in student productions. Learning by acting is a powerful method of instruction. Student actors must understand on an intellectual level the content of the performance and connect emotionally to their characters, who are set in a time, place, and social context. These different understandings need to be synthesized in a performance with an actor's body and voice. Acting, as an immersion exercise, forces an intimate relationship between information and personal experience.

When students are required to act, you will want to give the actors and directors some helpful hints. Impress upon the student actors that they are the interpreters of the script and that it is up to them to convey the text, emotion, and action of the script. The student directors help the actors make this happen.

For the actors to understand their characters and their roles in the production, some background research may be necessary. Students will need to understand the setting's social, political, and religious milieu. The more understanding the students have of the setting, the easier it will be for them to recreate appropriately a character's behavior. The clearer this character exists in an actor's imagination, the more effortless it will be to act the part. For this reason, it is easier for the students to portray characters and situations in time periods that are more familiar to them. However, for educational purposes, you may want students to learn about a period that is unfamiliar to them.

In addition to understanding their characters and the cultural context of the setting, the actors will have to understand the storyline. Every production will have conflicts and resolutions. The actors should identify the conflicts in which their characters are involved and what is at stake.

Once the actors master their various characters and the storyline, they will need to bring energy to their performances to make the video entertaining. A technique used by actors to add energy to their performances is to use a louder-than-normal voice, which subsequently forces a higher energy level into body movements. Once that energy is infused into the movements, actors attempt to return to a normal voice level but maintain the energy in their movements (Adler 1988, 10).

Body language is the primary communicator in face-to-face exchanges, while the spoken words are actually of secondary importance. In silent films, communication between the actors and audience was expressed almost exclusively through physical movements. Body language, rather than spoken dialogue, conveys the message with amazing success. In video acting, body movements may sometimes need to be exaggerated, especially if the actor is viewed from a distance in a long shot. However, body movements can also be very subtle and highlighted through close-ups or special camera angles.

DIRECTING ACTORS

Directors are responsible for helping actors perform according to the script or plan. Some directors choose to be involved to the point of requesting specific movements, facial expressions, and gestures. Other directors allow the actors to express themselves and only interject when they consider a change of course is needed. It will be up to the students to choose their desired method of directing, and it may change in reaction to the talent with which they are working. In any case, directors always get involved when the actors need help interpreting their roles.

A director can use the following techniques to help actors:

- Give the actors a vision of the scene.
- Identify the emotion of the scene for the actors.
- Let the actors improvise the scene.
- Give the actors verbs that describe the action of the scene (i.e., she is *admonishing*, he is *evading*, they are *grieving*).
- Have the actors paraphrase the scene.
- Give the actors the subtext of the scene (what the characters are thinking when they deliver their lines).
- Give the actors an image, complete with visual and auditory cues, on which to focus (i.e., "You are angry enough to have steam coming out your nostrils," and "Drink in the appearance of your true love as if she were your favorite fragrance").

Directors are also responsible for the positions of the actors and their movements in what is known as stage blocking. Each scene must be scripted as to where the actors stand and any movement they make. It is also up to the director to determine camera placement, movement, and angle in relation to the movement of the actors.

In addition to helping the actors and determining camera directions, the director should take care to choose appropriate costumes, props, and sets. If the production is pieced together over a period of days, the director will also need to ensure consistency in clothing, lighting, and scenery from day to day. It is distracting for the audience if the actors are suddenly transformed by different clothing and hairstyles from one shot to the next in the same scene. An easy way to avoid this situation is to encourage the students to leave everything they need for the production at school.

DRESS/COSTUMING

Dress is one way in which individuals express their identity. A discussion about the way clothing communicates can take place in the context of a lesson about video communication. How actors dress for a video can have a huge impact on how effectively their message is received, and talent in video should dress according to their part in the production. For example, if the students are making a video on lab safety, they should look like scientists and wear white lab coats, which lend credibility. If the students are producing a video on the stock market, they will command more respect from their audience if they are wearing business clothing rather than shorts and flip-flops.

Costuming is the dressing of a character for a theatrical performance. Having actors dress in period attire adds authenticity to any performance. Costuming can also liberate the actors to play their part more enthusiastically or realistically. Students are more likely to act like clowns if they are cloaked in fright wigs, gunnysacks, and huge shoes. If a character is portrayed as cool, it is easier for the student to play the part wearing dark shades and a leather jacket. If you want to free students for slapstick roles, give them the cover of outrageous outfits, wigs, and glasses. Costuming can have the effect of making an actor less self-conscious, allowing the character in the attire to emerge.

Some colors and patterns work better on video than others. When choosing costumes or clothing for a production, try several combinations if you have time. Stay away from small patterns and pinstripes, as they shift and move unnaturally on video. Solid colors work well, but bright white clothing under strong lights can sometimes glow and give a halo effect.

PROPS

The proper use of props in a video also adds an element of authenticity. Props help orient the audience to the action of the video, especially in theatrical performances. Props may also be necessary for demonstration purposes in a video, such as a ball in a video about gravitational acceleration. Props also give the actors something to do with their hands.

SYMBOLISM

Symbolism is an important communication tool in video. Just as in literature, video can have symbolic elements that suggest a meaning beyond their physical form. Symbols in video can be as obvious as a student coloring his or her thumb green to signify an affinity with plants or painting his or her hand gold to imply a golden touch. Metaphors are also useful in storytelling on video. The physical act of walking through fire to reach someone can be a metaphor for willingness to sacrifice or make a commitment. I have seen student projects that employ symbolism and metaphors overenthusiastically, most frequently video montages, in which symbols are sometimes used without meaning attached to them. Symbolism without purpose can be seen as free expression or abstract art, but it can also be very confusing to the viewer.

MUSIC

Adding a music score is an easy way to enhance almost any production, and students should be encouraged to add appropriate music to underscore their videos. Music is a master manipulator of emotion. It can be used to elicit whatever emotion the director or editor wishes as an effective communicator of mood and tone. Love scenes are frequently complemented by lyrical music, while scary scenes are punctuated by eerie music and noises.

Music can also convey ethnic and geographic information. Every culture has its signature music, and if this music is used in the video, the audience will identify the location. Bluegrass or country suggests rural America; rap, urban settings; sitars and chimes, India; chants and drums, Africa; and so on.

Students should match the music they choose to the mood of the video as well. Music can be used to change the mood of the video, with faster paced music heightening the energy or slower music bringing it down. The tempo of the music will dictate the timing of the cuts between images in the video.

Because music is such an effective communication vehicle, it must be chosen with great care. Popular music heard on the radio is copyright protected and therefore should not be used in commercially distributed videos without the written consent of the copyright holder. If there is any chance that the video will be shown on cable TV or sold for profit, proper rights for the music contained within should be secured. You can attempt to contact the publisher or owner of the rights directly or you can contact the American Society of Composers, Authors and Publishers (ASCAP) at www.ascap.com to secure onetime rights to a song for public distribution. All that said however, it is permissible for students to use popular songs for their class projects if the audience is limited to their class, friends, and family. The problem arises if the students want to show their video on public access cable or sell the video for profit. I ran into this problem when I created a music video for a faculty talent show that featured the male faculty dancing to a popular song. After its debut, enough people requested a copy that it became necessary to secure the proper rights to the song, which we are still attempting to do.

An alternative to dealing with intellectual property rights is to purchase royalty-free music, which is sold or distributed in many places. Freeplay Music (www.freeplay.com) has 2,100 titles in 35 genres that may be downloaded at no cost. The database of songs can be searched by CD, feel, style, and keywords. Digital Juice (www.digitaljuice.com) sells a 28-volume set of CDs for about $400; they contain all sorts of music from classical, to rock, to suspense, and even include wedding and sports music. Royalty Free Music (www.royaltyfreemusic.com) sells music at around $60 a CD; and Partners in Rhyme (www.partnersinrhyme.com) has CDs for about $40 a disk, as well as offering public domain sound effects. Royalty-free music is sometimes expensive, but it does allow you to distribute videos with professionally produced music.

Another free alternative to copyright music is to record original music from your school band or choir. Our fourth- and fifth-grade choir entered a contest for an Oscar Mayer hot dog commercial. The choir director helped the students establish a treatment, script, storyboard, and score for their commercial. Once the commercial was shot and edited, they recorded a live voice-over of an edited version of the Oscar Mayer jingle. The students were thrilled to have produced and performed in their own commercial.

SOUND EFFECTS

Sound effects are another means of auditory communication. Sound effects can add realism, punctuation, drama, or comic effect. In professionally produced videos, at minimum two channels of audio are recorded, one for the talent, another for ambient noises and sound effects. Ambient sound tracks add realism to a video and are usually only noticed when absent. Unfortunately, the digital video cameras that students will most likely use will only be able to record one track of audio. Therefore, ambient sound and sound effects may have to be recorded separately and added to the video in postproduction.

Recording sound effects is simple; use the camcorder to record the desired sound. With editing software you will be able to separate the soundtrack from the video and then add that soundtrack to another video requiring these sound effects. Another option is to record directly into the video using the voice-over feature in the editing software. Here you can actually watch the video track as you record an audio track into it. This is how the choir sang their jingle in perfect time to the images of the video. This is also how another group added the clatter of typewriter keys to letters that appeared in the opening credits of a video.

In addition to recording your own sound effects, you may want to use software programs with libraries of sound effects like dogs barking, trains whistling, wind blowing, and crowds cheering. For a more robust set of sounds, you will want to direct your students to the Internet or purchase a set of CDs that contain sound effects. Sound Dogs (www.sounddogs.com) has thousands of public domain (royalty-free) sound effects available for download at no cost. I have used this site to get a clanging school bell, a ringing telephone, and cheering crowds. I have use of a 60-CD set of sound effects from the BBC, which our theatre department bought for use in their productions and I borrow for student videos when necessary.

Distorting a sound is another form of sound effect. There are sound editing software tools that you can use to distort your voice so that it sounds as though the voice were being heard over a loudspeaker in a stadium or echoing off cavern walls. A low-tech free way to distort voices is to have students talk on walkie-talkies, record in a shower stall, or speak through a mailing tube.

CLASS ACTIVITY FOR STUDY OF TV COMMUNICATION

Video communicates through both sound and video. Frequently, however, the visual concept is underutilized, and the majority of the message is conveyed through the audio channel. When discussing message design and communication strategies for video, a useful exercise for the class is to watch videos with and without sound and with and without picture to see which channel communicates better.

For homework, have the students pick four different types of shows, for instance, news, sports, nature, sitcom, home shopping, documentary, drama, thriller, or commercial. Have them watch the first two minutes of the show with the volume off and see if they can understand what is going on; have them take notes about their ability to interpret the images. Then have them continue to watch the show with the volume turned up but with their eyes closed. Again, have them jot notes on what they can understand of the action from the soundtrack.

Lead a discussion in class about their experience. You will find that few TV shows are easily understood without the audio. Ask the students which of the two senses they think is more important for understanding TV based on their homework experience. You can broaden the discussion and ask which sense they think would be more debilitating to lose with respect to communicating with other people.

CONCLUSION

Video offers a rich array of communication possibilities for the students. The text of the script allows students to communicate through words, symbols, and metaphors. The visual aspects of video allow them to communicate through images, acting, costuming, and props. The auditory aspects allow them to communicate through music and sound effects. The combination of these three aspects provides limitless opportunities for student expression and message creation.

Chapter Three

Aesthetic Instruction

Video has great potential for communicating visually, but, as discussed in the previous chapter, the visual component of video is frequently under employed. Through simple instruction and demonstration, though, students can be taught to add greater depth to the visual dimension of their projects. Traditionally, aesthetic education has been the domain of art classes, but this form of instruction is increasingly necessary as our culture becomes more visually oriented and video establishes itself as the dominant mass communication medium.

The ability to construct an image that communicates a message is a highly valuable skill, not only for video production but for application technologies like PowerPoint, HyperStudio, Photoshop, and web design as well. Through the use of computers, today's students prepare more visual material than previous generations, and I am careful to include some aesthetic instruction in any course that involves visual content.

This chapter will explore the basics of aesthetic instruction through video imagery, starting with the composition of video footage using the Rule of Thirds and other picture composition guidelines. Then we will focus on the decisions that have to be made prior to shooting a video. Next, I will share a classroom exercise that simultaneously teaches students visual video communication strategies; the operation of the camera, microphone, and editing software; and the way in which a director manages a shoot in a studio using the proper terminology and procedures.

PICTURE COMPOSITION FOR VIDEO

Rule of Thirds

Some very basic rules exist for framing and shooting video; the most elementary concern is head and lead room. That is, human subjects should be framed in such a way that there is the right amount of room above their heads. If the subjects are in motion, there should be the right amount of room in front of them so that they do not keep bumping into the forward edge of the frame. To help gauge the appropriate amount of head and lead room, students should be taught the Rule of Thirds. Pictures should be divided into thirds by two imaginary, equally spaced "third lines" trisecting the picture both horizontally and vertically (figure 3.1). Key elements of the picture that the director wants the audience to focus on should be on these lines or at the intersections of the lines. When judging how much headroom to give a subject, draw an imaginary

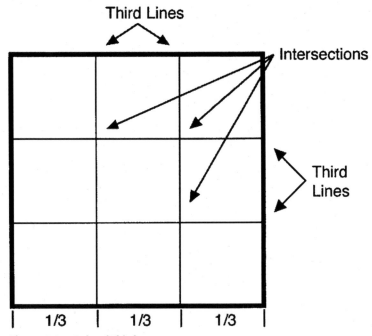

Figure 3.1   Rule of Thirds

Divide the picture frame into thirds and place important elements of the picture on the third lines or at the intersections.

Figure 3.2   Rule of Thirds

Here the Rule of Thirds is applied to this picture where the
dominant element of the girls resides on the third lines and
at its intersections.

line delineating the top third of the viewfinder and put the subject's eyes
on that line (figure 3.2). When judging how much lead room to give a
moving subject, place the subject on the vertical third line so that the
subject is moving from the edge of the frame into the open space to-
wards the other third line (figure 3.3).

The Rule of Thirds applies to the composition of all images, both
moving and still. It is a more interesting way to compose a picture than
simply placing all the action and focal points of the picture in the center. Once you and your students are made aware of the Rule of Thirds,
you will notice that most professionally produced video and still images obey the Rule of Thirds. One example is newscasts, which position an anchorperson on the left third and a superimposed still image
or icon at the intersection of the right and top third lines (figure 3.4).
Video footage of landscapes also adheres to the Rule of Thirds, by placing the horizon either on the top third and focusing on the flora and
fauna, or on the bottom third of the picture and focusing on the sky

Figure 3.3   Leadroom for Moving Subject

When judging leadroom for a moving subject, place the moving subject so that there is space in the frame into which the subject can move.

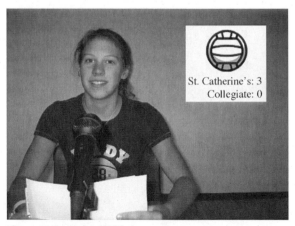

Figure 3.4   Rule of Thirds

Notice how the traditional position of an anchorperson obeys the Rule of Thirds.

Figure 3.5   Horizon on Top Third

When the horizon is on the top third of the picture, the focus is on the landscape below. Credit: Berkley Blanchard

(figures 3.5 and 3.6). This framing of the horizon is known as the classical solution.

Field of View

Field of view, another basic concept in picture composition, refers to how much of the subject you can see in a given frame (figure 3.7).

- The extreme long shot (XLS), otherwise known as an establishing shot, provides the viewer with a panoramic view in which the subject may not be distinguishable in any detail. The shot places the subject in his or her surroundings.
- The long shot (LS) is also considered an establishing shot in that it identifies the subject in his or her surroundings, but it allows for more detail because the subject is not as small as he or she would be in an XLS. The XLS and LS are two shots used to highlight surroundings and not the subject.

Figure 3.6   Horizon on Bottom Third

When the horizon is on the bottom third of the picture, the focus is on the landscape above. Credit: Brian Ward

- The medium shot (MS) crops the subject somewhere between the knees and waist. Here the subject is placed in the context of his or her surroundings, but most of the attention of the viewer will be on the subject.
- The medium close-up (MCU), also known as the head and shoulders shot, is the most popular video shot. This shot is used repeatedly in

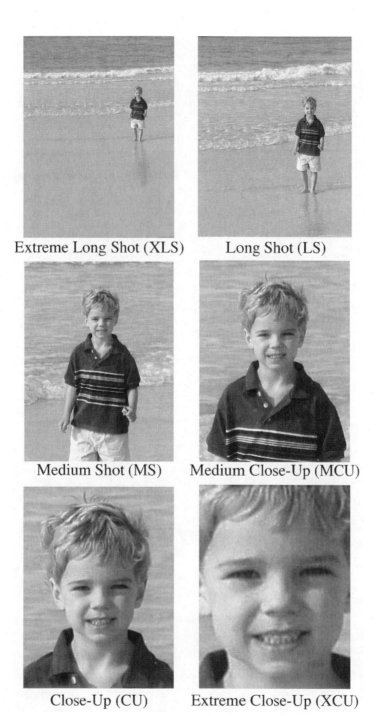

Figure 3.7   Field of Views; Credit: Mike Nerny

many video genres because it gives details about the subject's face while not invading the personal space of the subject.

- The close-up (CU) almost fills the entire screen with the subject's face, which allows for great facial detail. In this shot, almost no detail of the subject's surroundings is available, as the focus is completely on the subject.
- The extreme close-up (XCU) fills the screen with an unnaturally close view. This shot invades the personal space of the subject and minute details are highlighted, which the camera operator blatantly forces the viewer to consider.

If the students choose their field of view shots appropriately and use the Rule of Thirds to place the subjects in the frame of the picture, they can shoot professional-looking footage. Strict adherence to these rules will prevent subjects being cut off at the ankles or missing the tops of their heads. As with most rules, these are made to be broken, though students should be careful not to violate these rules unless they have a reason. A rule violated calls attention to itself, and if that is not the intended purpose

Figure 3.8   Converging Lines

Converging lines draws the attention of the viewer to the intersection of the lines. Credit: Brian Ward

of the violation, it will only serve to distract the audience. Encourage your students to understand and use the rules but be careful not to discourage creativity, fresh perspectives, and original ideas.

Backgrounds

The surroundings of the subject can add or subtract from the aesthetic effect of the composition. Converging lines within a picture's background can draw the attention of the viewer to a focal point that the director chooses (figure 3.8). Frames within a frame can act to isolate a subject. Notice how in figure 3.9 your attention is drawn to the boy framed by the railroad tracks.

Backgrounds can also distract viewers from the subject if they are too busy or contain elements that compete for attention with the intended subject of the video (figure 3.10). The cameraperson should take care to notice what is behind the subject to avoid "false attachments" to foreign objects in the background, for instance the antenna that seems to be growing out of the subject's head in figure 3.11.

Figure 3.9   Frames within a Frame

Lines within a picture can serve to frame and draw attention to the subject. Credit: William Bagole

Figure 3.10   Distracting Background

If the background is too busy, it can be distracting.

Figure 3.11   False Attachments

Be careful not to have things behind the subject look as though they are growing out of the subject's head.

SHOOTING PROFESSIONAL-LOOKING VIDEO

A thousand decisions have to be made when capturing images on video. Knowing what choices are available and what effect they have on the video is what aesthetic instruction for video is all about.

The following choices need to be made when shooting:

- What is visible in the shot?
  - The subject's eyes in an extreme close-up?
  - The subject's head in a close-up?
  - The subject and his/her surroundings in a long shot?
  - Two people talking in a two shot (defined later in chapter)?
  - A scenic panorama in an extreme long shot?
- Where should the camera be placed in relation to the subject(s)?
  - Above, below, or level with the subject(s)?
  - In front, behind, or off to the side of the subject(s)?
- How will the camera move, and the perspective change, during the shot?
  - Will the perspective stay the same?
  - Will the camera move closer or zoom in on a portion of the picture?
  - Will the camera move away or zoom out to include more information?
- What is the perspective of the camera going to be?
  - Is the camera representing the perspective of an objective observer not part of the action?
  - Or is it representing the perspective of an individual who is taking part in the action?
- What parts of the picture should be in focus?
  - The entire picture is in focus?
  - The subject is in focus, but the background and foreground out of focus?
  - The entire picture is out of focus?
- How much light is in the picture and where is it coming from?
  - Is it dark or overly bright?
  - Is the light coming from behind, in front, above, below, or all around?
- Will the camera be steady or shaky?
  - Will the camera be mounted on a tripod and therefore steady with smooth motion?
  - Or will the camera be handheld and shaky with jerky, uneven movements?

Once the footage has been taken and the video is being edited, other aesthetic decisions need to be made (technical terms are defined later in the chapter):

- What special effects, if any, should be added to a clip?
    - Strobe or ghost trail effect?
    - Black and white, sepia, or other color balance manipulations?
    - Reverse the direction of the clip to play backwards?
    - Speed the clip up or slow it down?
- How long should video clips be?
    - Short clips that jump back and forth resulting in quick action and fast pacing?
    - Long clips pieced together resulting in slowed action and a leisurely pace?
- What types of transitions should connect the clips?
    - Simple cut from one clip to another?
    - Fade in and fade out?
    - Cross dissolve clips into each other?

CLASSROOM EXERCISE FOR TEACHING COMMUNICATION THROUGH VIDEO IMAGES

Each decision the students make in response to the list of questions above will have a visual impact. The best way I have found to help the students answer these questions is through class participation, demonstration, and discussion.

I turn the classroom into a video studio where I am the director and the students are the talent, camera operators, audio operators, and technical directors. Together, we shoot many similar scenes, changing only one aspect of the video at a time, and then evaluate its impact on the video. The exercise is highly participatory, and the students learn how to use the video equipment and editing software as they work on the footage. By using the students as talent, I put their favorite actors on display. By acting as the director of the shoot, I model the proper protocols, procedures, and jargon of an authentic video shoot (more on production protocols, procedures, and jargon in chapter 6). This is a highly effective lesson, as the students discover for themselves how small changes in camera angle can have a subtle but significant impact on the viewer's interpretation.

To turn the classroom into a video studio, I set up the DV camcorder on a tripod with a long Firewire cable connected to a computer running the digital editing software. The computer is also connected to a LCD projector that projects the computer image onto a large screen, allowing the whole class to watch the video being captured and edited on the computer (figure 3.12). I spend time explaining all the pieces of equipment, how they are connected, and what we are going to do with them. By connecting the DV camera directly to the computer, I can send footage from the camera to the computer's hard drive and review the footage on the computer screen instantaneously. In this manner I can quickly capture similar scenes, changing one visual aspect at a time for a back-to-back comparison and discussion.

For each sequence of scenes, I pick different students for each function: a camera operator to aim, focus, and frame the picture; an audio operator to hold the microphone near the action; a technical director to operate the computer, and capture and play back the footage; and as many actors as the scene needs. I direct this makeshift video crew's efforts by giving the lines and direction to the talent and telling the camera operator what shot

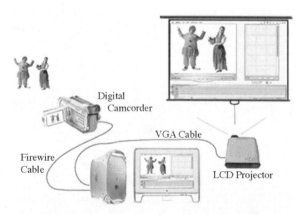

Figure 3.12   Computer Setup for Classroom Exercise

Connect the digital video camera to the computer and the computer to a digital projector. Use the digital video editing software to control the camera and the projector to show the whole class how to use the software.

I want and how it should be framed. I also tell the technical director, who is at the controls of the computer, when to start capturing the footage to the hard drive, which clips to play back, and what effects to add. To really go all out, I include a person to snap the clapstick to identify the scene and take.

The rest of the class observes a working video crew, becoming familiar with the respective roles and learning the operational flow of a shoot. When the scenes are captured, differing only in one aspect, and played back to back, the whole class participates in a discussion about the effect that one change has on the feel of the video. Ultimately, the discussion focuses on what is communicated to the audience through the decisions a director makes.

The modules that follow are ways to demonstrate various visual effects. It takes time to set the stage for the actors, successfully record the action, review the series of clips, and then discuss the results. You will not be able to complete the entire list of modules below in a single marathon lesson. It is best to pick three to five of the following modules per 50-minute lesson.

The first set of modules deals with decisions and changes that affect the camera's perspective. These decisions are made at the time the action is captured on the camera. The second set of modules deals with changes that are made to the footage after it has been captured, using digital manipulation and adding special effects.

This exercise always leads to giggling, humor, and high interest. Having the students act on camera in front of the class will cause the most jaded of high schoolers to blush and have trouble containing their excitement. So prepare yourself for fun and constructive chaos. You are the director and you call the shots, literally!

CAPTURING THE ACTION AND
COMMUNICATING THROUGH VIDEO IMAGES

The camera becomes the eyes of the audience, and with it the director has great control over the viewer's relationship to the action and characters. The perspective of the camera is the perspective of the audience, and the viewers are forced to see the action the way the director dictates. Where the camera is in relation to the subjects and action and with what clarity the action has been recorded can have a powerful effect on the viewer's interpretation of the story. Here are some of the exercises I use to demonstrate these effects.

Camera Angle

The three basic camera angles are low, on-level, and high, and each angle conveys a different feel. Low camera angles, when the camera is below the subject looking up, make the subject appear taller, bigger, and more powerful. This camera angle places the viewer in a submissive position relative to the subject. On-level camera angles have a neutral effect on the subject and viewer's interpretation. High camera angles, when the camera is looking down on a subject, make the subject look shorter and less important, and place the viewer in a position of dominance over the subject.

To demonstrate this, I choose a camera operator, technical director, audio operator, and three students for talent—one short, one average, and one tall. I then shoot three short scenes, one with each student, in which each delivers one line, "You're in trouble," and shakes a finger at the camera. I capture the talent delivering the line three different ways. With the stout student, the scene is shot from a low camera angle, the camera almost touching the floor, with the talent looking down at the camera. For the average height student, the camera is on level, the student looking directly at the camera. For the taller student, a high camera angle is used with the talent looking up at the camera (this may involve the camera operator having to stand on a chair and hold the camera over his or her head).

Using the editing software, play the clips back to back. Discuss with the class how the camera angle can make a person appear taller or shorter. Ask the students which scene makes them feel the most threatened. This is not a scientific experiment in which all other variables are held constant, so the audience may be swayed by factors other than camera angles, such as a more convincing delivery by one actor. For a more controlled experiment, you may want to run the scenes again from the three different camera angles using the same actor delivering the same line.

Field of View and Zooming

The amount of information that is in the field of view of the camera is another way in which the viewer's perspective is controlled and understanding can be manipulated. The audience can be forced to notice

whatever the director wants them to by zooming in on the important element of the scene. In this way, the director can control the audience's
attention to details.

Zooms are rarely used in professional productions, as discussed in
chapter 6; they prefer instead to take close-ups of important elements and
edit these scenes into the video later. However, in single-camera field productions such as those created by your students, zooms can be used to
change the field of view without having to splice scenes together in the
editing phase. Your students will need no encouragement to use the zoom
on the camera and you should preface this exercise with a caution against
using too much zooming.

This exercise shows the students how the director can focus the
viewer's attention by changing the field of view using a zoom and a skit
with two actors and a book.

The first take of this exercise consists of two actors standing on either
side of a book that is propped up on a table in a two shot—two people in
the shot (figure 3.13). Looking at the camera, talent 1 delivers the line,

Figure 3.13   A Two Shot

"Today we are going to read the book (name of book) by (author of book)." Talent 2 then turns from talent 1 toward the camera and delivers the line, "(Name of book) is about (storyline of book)." During this first take, the camera stays with the same two shot throughout.

The second take of the same scene involves changing the field of view to focus the viewer's attention on the book. In this take the actors deliver the same lines, the camera beginning with the same two shot; but halfway through talent 2's explanation of the storyline, the camera zooms in to a close-up of the book cover.

Watch the two clips back to back and discuss how the camera controls the perspective of an audience. Discuss how the director can use close-ups and extreme close-ups to force the audience to notice or focus on details. Ask the students which of the two clips is more interesting to watch and why. Discuss how the movement of the camera reflects a change of interest in the subject and involves the audience in that change.

Point of View of the Camera

Cameras can be used in such a way that they are observers of the action, "objective cameras," or participants in the action, "subjective cameras." Through these two different camera angles, the director can control the audience's sense of involvement in the story. The objective camera places the audience in a voyeuristic and detached position, while the subjective camera makes the audience feel a part of the action.

A way to demonstrate these two camera perspectives is to have a student explain on video how to make a paper airplane. To demonstrate the objective camera, pick two actors, one who knows how to make a paper airplane, and position the camera in a two shot with the actors facing each other (figure 3.14). In the first take, have the first actor explain to the second how to make a paper airplane, both verbally and through demonstration.

To demonstrate the subjective camera in the second take, use only the first actor and position the camera just over his or her shoulder, pointing it at his or her hands (figure 3.15). In this take, have the actor narrate how to make a paper airplane and simultaneously demonstrate. This will give the viewer the exact perspective of the person making the airplane, and the audience will feel like participants because the narrator is speaking directly to them.

Figure 3.14 A Two Shot of Students Facing Each Other

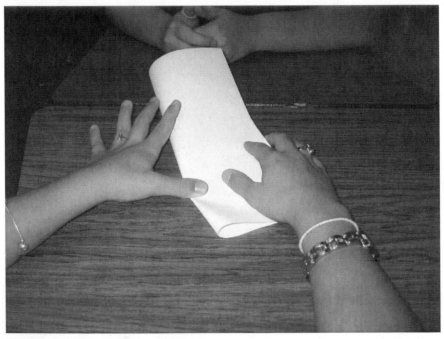

Figure 3.15 A Point of View (POV) Shot

Discuss the difference in camera views and ask the students which take they liked better for the purpose of learning how to make a paper airplane. Ask them which camera angle caught and held their attention more. List with them instances in which they think one camera angle would be more effective than the other.

Lighting

Lighting is one of the more difficult aspects for students to master in video. Very often they will shoot a subject against a bright background that makes the subject appear dark like a silhouette, though this can also be a desired special effect. The following exercise demonstrates how light can change the mood of a shot and how a light background will effect the camera's ability to record a subject.

Have an actor stand with his or her back to the window on a bright sunny day. If you do not have a window or it is not a sunny day, have the actor stand in front of a lamp or some other source of light so that the light is behind them. Have the actor deliver the line "Do you know who I am?" on tape. Next, position the camera so that the light source is in front of the talent and the background is dark. Have the talent deliver the same line on tape.

Play the two clips back to back and be sure to point out that the subject's features are not visible on camera when the light source is behind the subject: the camera compensates for the bright background by darkening the foreground. Explain to the students that, if they want to light the subject's face, the light source must be in front, reflecting the light toward the camera. Editing software is able to compensate somewhat for poor light values on tape, but for best results and the least hassle, students should capture well-lit footage on camera and not rely on manipulations in postproduction.

Discuss the different moods created by altered light values. Ask the students which lighting makes the subject seem nefarious. The darker scene should evoke a more sinister feeling.

Focus

Both the degree of focus and portions of the image in focus affect message delivery. Less expensive digital video cameras, like the ones your students may be using, do not have many options for focus. They all have a manual focus option, but most do not allow you to change the depth of field to control how much of the picture is in focus. Most of the cameras your students will be using are designed to get as much of the picture in focus as possible in what is called deep focus.

You can switch the camera to manual focus and make the entire picture slightly out of focus in what is called soft focus. Soft focus can create a dreamlike, foggy, or surreal setting. It can also communicate a character's confusion or disorientation. From a cosmetic standpoint, a soft focus can also blur small facial blemishes or wrinkles.

To demonstrate the effect of soft focus, stage two takes of the same scene, one using sharp focus, the other using soft. The scene for both takes is an actor who is lying asleep, and who slowly wakes up, rubs his or her eyes, gets up, and exits stage left. In the first take, have the camera operator maintain a sharp, deep focus throughout the entire clip. In the second take, have the camera operator switch to manual focus and start with a soft focus. As the actor rubs his or her eyes, have the camera operator bring the picture into focus.

Watch both clips and ask the students if the soft focus changed their perspective or involvement in the picture. Did the soft focus communicate the feeling you get when you wake up? What other times might you want the picture to be out of focus?

Dress and Body Language

As discussed in chapter 2, another way to communicate is through costumes or dress and body language. In the following exercise I have one actor deliver the same line dressed in different outfits and using different body language. In the first take I have the actor dress in a smart business jacket and spectacles and say with confidence, "It is my opinion that the economy is slowing and the stock market is going to go down." In the second take, have the same actor dress in a Hawaiian shirt, baseball hat, sunglasses, and headset, delivering the same line but in an offhand, cavalier, or even humorous manner.

Discuss with the class their reactions to the two different messages. Which scene was more convincing? What factors influenced their confidence in one persona over the other?

Shaky Cam versus Steady Cam

One of the most obvious indications that a video is an amateur production is the "shaky cam" effect caused by holding the camera in the hand instead of using a tripod, dolly, or some other image stabilization equipment. Professionals do use the shaky cam, however, to communicate a loss of control, panic, or disorientation.

To demonstrate the shaky cam's suggestion of disorientation, pick an actor who will look into the lens of the camera in a close-up shot and ask, "Are you all right?" For the first take, mount the camera on a tripod. For the second take, have the camera operator hand hold the camera, add a small amount of movement, and have the actor repeat the same line.

Watch both clips and discuss which one creates the impression that the character being addressed is ill. Ask the students if they have seen the shaky cam used on broadcast TV or in the movies. If so, how did it make them feel? Have the students discuss appropriate occasions for using the shaky, as opposed to the stable, cam.

COMMUNICATION THROUGH VIDEO MANIPULATION

When the camera is connected to the computer and the computer is projecting that image in front of the class, you can shoot multiple takes of a similar scene for side-by-side comparison, as in the previous exercises. It also allows you to apply special effects to captured video for instant analysis, and to study each effect's communicative value. Once the video footage is captured on the computer, it can be duplicated and that copy manipulated using digital effects in the editing software. The two clips can be played back to back as an almost instant comparison of the original and manipulated footage.

The editing program you are using will dictate what special effects are available to demonstrate. iMovie2 has twelve special effects included, with the possibility of adding others with Virtix and GeeThree.com (more on iMovie plug-ins in chapter 6). Pinnacle's Studio DV version 7 software can strobe and change the speed of the film.

Speed of Film

Changing the speed of the film to accelerate or slow the action has a predictable effect on the video. In almost all cases, speeding up the film adds humor, while slowing down the film adds drama. To demonstrate this effect, choose three or four students to be videotaped running in place. Have them make pained faces, brush their foreheads, and jostle for position while they run in place for about a minute. Once captured in the editing software, duplicate the clip two times so that you have a total of three identical clips. Leave the first video clip as the control for the experiment. Speed up the second video to three or four times the original speed. Slow the third down to one quarter of its original speed. Play the three clips back to back.

Note the reaction of the class. I can guarantee that the accelerated footage will make the class laugh. The slowed footage will also elicit some laughs, but the drawn out wiping of the brows and the pained expressions add drama to the clip. Discuss with the students how the speed of the clip changed their perception of the action. Which clip makes the actors look as if they are trying harder? What would happen if you sped up the film and then slowed it down? Compare the effects of changing the speed of video footage.

Transitions

Every editing package has options for transitioning from one clip to another, and each transition communicates in its own way. A simple cut from one clip to the next is a neutral transition that does not necessarily communicate anything to the audience. A fade-in from black signifies a beginning, while a fade-out to black communicates an end. A cross dissolve, in which the first clip begins the fade-out, while the next clip appears to fade in, is a smooth transition that signifies continuity. The second clip appears a logical next step.

To demonstrate these transitions you will need more clips. You will sequence them with the clip of students running that you shot to illustrate the film speed special effect. This is your opportunity to give the active students who have been squirming in their seats a chance to exercise and burn off energy. You will need at least two more actors to be videotaped doing jumping jacks, push-ups, sit-ups, or any other type of exercise. Capture two or more 15-second clips of students exercising.

Sequence the clips on the timeline in the editing program (explained in chapter 6) without any transitions. Run the video and call attention to the cuts between clips. Now add different transitions between the clips and play it again. Discuss how these transitions affect the viewer's anticipation of what is to follow. How effectively does the video flow from one clip to another using the various transitions? Discuss which transitions are appropriate for what types of video and context.

Music and Voice-Overs Revisited

In the editing software, you can also add music and voice-overs. As discussed in chapter 2, music can have a profound effect on the mood and interpretation of a video clip. To demonstrate this, it is useful to have music CDs on hand to add to the captured clips. Have your students bring in music and add it to the different clips you have captured as part of this exercise. Have music of different tempos and genres to add to the clips, and discuss the various effects the music has on the audience's perception of the video. Use the voice-over feature of the software to narrate off camera the running-in-place race, and discuss how effective it is to have someone explain the action on the screen.

CONCLUSION

The exercises discussed in this chapter are a fun, high-energy, active way to teach students about video aesthetics. Students will also get a feel for how to use a nonlinear editing software program, how to operate a digital video camera, and how to work as a video team under a director in an authentic video shoot. It may take several sessions to complete every module listed in this chapter, but the lessons are well worth teaching. At the very least, the exercises are an enjoyable way to introduce the software and camera to the class.

The demonstrations and discussions will introduce students to the many options available to them for delivering their message visually, and they will be much better prepared to make the decisions necessary to add depth to the visual dimension of their videos.

Chapter Four

Preproduction

Preproduction is the first phase in the production process. In preproduction an idea is proposed, a concept is adopted, the message is designed, a script is written, and a plan for the production is formalized. This is a critical phase and the more time spent planning, the smoother the production and more effective the video will be. Professionals estimate that they spend 80 percent of their time in preproduction!

During this phase, your students will design an effective message for a target audience, following the principles discussed in chapter 2. You will want the students to think about how they are going to communicate to their audience through video and what type of music, costuming, props, sound effects, and symbolism they will use to reinforce their message. All of these topics are covered in detail in chapter 2.

It is sometimes difficult to convince students of the importance of planning for their production. To impress the importance on my students, I require they at least turn in a Student Video Project Proposal (figure 2.1). For some projects, I also require that the students turn in a written treatment, a script, storyboards, or a shot list. Assigning any one of the mentioned elements helps ensure your students will put forth the effort necessary to be successful in the subsequent production and postproduction phases of their projects. This process follows the same logic English teachers use when requiring note cards, outlines, and rough drafts to be turned in during a research paper assignment.

STUDENT VIDEO PROJECT PROPOSAL FORM

On the Student Video Project Proposal form (figures 1.1 and 2.1 are available on the website) students are forced to commit to a purpose, an audience, a genre, elements, equipment, locations, and a schedule. The members of the crew are assigned responsibilities, and a distribution format is selected. This form should be turned in to you and approved with a signature. You should maintain a copy and check on the progress of projects to make sure they stay on schedule. I also post a copy of this form on a corkboard labeled "Projects in Process" next to the corkboards used to reserve and check out equipment so that students can see what other projects are going on in the school and plan their production accordingly.

Title, Purpose, and Audience

The title, purpose, and audience lines on the form require that the students give their project a title, think about the desired outcome of their video, and identify a target audience. These decisions are critical to designing an effective message, as discussed in chapter 2. As the students go on to create their video, they should be constantly thinking, "Does this accomplish the purpose of this video?" and "Will this appeal to my target audience?"

Genres

When the students have identified their title, purpose, and audience, they must then decide on the treatment. A treatment is a statement identifying, in general terms, the storyline, characters, informational content, locations, and dominant images of the video. If you choose to have the students turn in a treatment, as discussed in chapter 2, it should be between 80 and 150 words.

On the Student Video Project Proposal form, the students will report their treatment in terms of Genre and Elements. Identifying the treatment will, in turn, indicate the production style (more on production styles in chapter 2). The presentational genre, in which actors talk to the audience, is usually used in educational programs, documentaries, news broadcasts, kids' videos, commercials, and game shows. The realistic genre, in which talent act as though the camera is not there, is found in entertainment films and reality TV, and comedy genres. The expressionistic genre, in which symbolic imagery and music are used to convey a message, is commonly found in music videos and video montages. Of course, any production can contain elements of one or all of the styles; but, for the most part, the above will hold true.

Elements

On the Student Video Project Proposal form, the students will also report the various elements they anticipate they will use in their video. Going through the elements list helps the students realize what possibilities are available to them. They can conduct interviews, record actual events (live action), or stage a performance. For sound beyond what has been recorded by the camera, they can import music or record their own narration. In addition to the footage captured by the camera, they can import video footage (imported video) from another source such as a VHS tape, digital video disk (DVD), or the Internet. They can import still images or take video of pictures; create their own pixilation, taking a series of still images of an object that is moved incrementally and then sequencing them to make it appear as though the object is moving; or use virtual reality video footage, which can be most easily obtained by videotaping a video game.

The thought of using video game footage did not occur to me until some students opened their foreign film with footage of a video game character who was lost in Sydney, Australia. They dubbed the footage with French-language narration. The video character dissolved into a live character holding the same pose standing on a similar-looking street. It turned out to be a very effective way to place the character in another country by using virtual reality.

In postproduction the students can also add titles and text, graphics, and special effects. I usually go through some of the effects available to them when I am explaining to the students how to fill out this form; that way they can think about what effects they might use to enhance their video.

Equipment Needs

The students also need to identify their equipment needs in the preproduction process. They will, of course, need a digital video camcorder (DV camcorder), DV tapes, and a DV editing computer, but I list these items on the form to remind them that they need to reserve this equipment ahead of time. Other equipment on the form can be reserved and checked out as needed, such as microphones, tripods, dollies, lights, reflectors, external hard drives, and clappers.

I have established a reservation-and-checkout system using the Digital Video Equipment Reservation/Checkout Form (figure 4.1). I have three corkboards labeled Reserved, Checked Out, and Projects in Process. If the students are reserving equipment, which they are encouraged to do as early as possible, given the first-come-first-served policy, they fill out the form and place it on the reservation board. The form has a date and time reserved line that establishes a priority order for equipment. If the students do not show up by 3:45 PM to claim their equipment, they lose their reservation, and the equipment can be loaned out to another group.

Digital Video Equipment Reservation/Checkout Form

Date/Time Needed: _____

Date/Time Reserved: _____

Date Due Back: _____ @ 1:30 (After 3:45 work hours will be assigned)

Student's Name: _____

Grade: _____

For Class: _____ Teacher: _____

Official Use Only

Signed Out By: _____

Date/Time Out: _____

Signed In By: _____

Date/Time In: _____

❑ DV Cam _____   ❑ DV Tape # _____   ❑ Tripod _____
  ❑ Case   ❑ Video Cable   ❑ Microphone   ❑ Handle
  ❑ Power Adt ❑ FW Cable   ❑ Handheld _____ ❑ Pan Head
  ❑ Battery   ❑ Light/Flash   ❑ Lavaliere _____ ❑ Case
  ❑ Remote   ❑ Floppy Adapter   ❑ Boom _____ ❑ Dolly _____
  ❑ Manual   ❑ PC Card   ❑ Clapstick/Slate _____
  ❑ Lens Cover ❑ Memory Stick _____ ❑ Firewire HD _____
  ❑ Strap

❑ Other: _____

Please Read: I understand that this equipment is to be used in support of academic events only and that equipment must be picked up and returned on time. I accept full responsibility for ANY equipment I have checked out that is damaged, lost, or stolen. Equipment returned late will result in work hours assigned.

Signature: _____ Date: _____

Figure 4.1 Equipment Reservation/Checkout Form

Also in the equipment needed section of the Student Video Project Proposal form are costumes, sets, and props lines. Here the students are encouraged to think of what items they will need for their production and begin to plan for their acquisition.

Locations

Some student productions will need to be shot on location. On the locations line, the students will list the sites they anticipate using. Here you will be able to guide them either by making sure that they can get to the location(s) listed or by suggesting alternative sites.

Schedule

Establishing a schedule is one of the most important parts of preproduction. Because video productions are group efforts, scheduling is made more difficult by the demands and complexity of the students' busy lives. Projects have to be scheduled in advance to give students an opportunity either to find common times to meet or to rearrange their schedules. More often than not, weekends offer the only free time in common; and, consequently, demands on video equipment during the weekends can be very heavy.

I encourage the students, while establishing a schedule, to work backwards from the due date and set three completion dates: preproduction, production, and postproduction. I encourage them to set a postproduction completion time before their project due date to give themselves a cushion. This extra time also allows them to fine-tune the video. Once a detailed schedule for their project is set, I encourage them to reserve the necessary equipment.

Distribution Format

It is important to think about a distribution format when planning a video, for several reasons. First, if you plan to distribute a video over the web or on CD ROM, it is important to use lots of close-up shots and make any text that must be read larger than usual, because the video will be significantly reduced in size when it is compressed in these two formats. If there is to be any hope of reading a facial expression or understanding a text, they will have to be in extreme close-up and large text to compensate for the smaller window size.

Second, if you use DVD as a distribution format, it opens nonlinear opportunities. You can break a video into parts that can be viewed in any order, as opposed to the linear nature of other, tape-based, systems that run from beginning to end.

Archiving

If there is any possibility that the students might go back and reedit the video in the future, and your computer is equipped with a DVD burner, it is useful to archive the raw computer files on a data DVD disk. A data DVD disk is a 4.7-gigabyte (GB) CD ROM that is large enough to hold the computer files of average student projects. Before copying the computer files to a blank DVD disk, make sure the folder or directory containing the project is smaller than 4.7 GB. Once the files are copied, you can delete the project folder from the hard drive, making room for the next project. To edit the archived project, copy the contents of the data DVD disk back to the computer's hard drive.

Archiving video projects any other way is difficult given the large size of the files. Few other options exist that are as inexpensive as DVD disks. Unfortunately, the disks are still relatively expensive at about $5 per disk. The only other option for backing up video files is a tape backup system, involving expensive hardware, software, and tapes.

Crew

Assigning crew responsibilities at the beginning is essential. Each member must know his or her tasks. Crew responsibilities are discussed further in chapter 5.

Approval

The Student Video Project Proposal form should be turned in to you before production begins. Have students submit this form during a pitch meeting, at which they approach you with their idea as if they were trying to secure funding for their project, or sell it to you as if you were a TV station executive. Meet with the entire crew and listen to their ideas. Have them explain their vision for the project and judge whether their goal is feasible and whether it meets your expectations. If the ideas are sketchy, have them flesh out their concepts; help them if necessary.

You may want them to turn in a written treatment as described earlier in this chapter and in chapter 2. A written treatment will force them to formalize a concept, ensuring that they do not come to the meeting with little more than vague notions.

After you approve the concept, make sure the students have a detailed schedule that coordinates crew, equipment, and locations. It takes a great deal of organization to pull off a video project; and, as we are all aware, many students struggle in this area. Check their plan to see if they have allowed enough time for each phase, and be sure that they reserve the equipment so that it will be there when they need it. You may also want to establish times you will meet with them to check on their progress.

At the end of the meeting, if you are satisfied, sign off on the project, make a copy of the form for yourself, and return the form to the group. I post this form next to the reservation board mentioned earlier so that others are aware of the projects taking place and can plan accordingly.

STORYBOARDS

Storyboarding a production is an effective way to give a script or treatment a visual dimension by illustrating major scenes of the production in serial fashion, much like a cartoon strip. The exercise of drawing visuals in a storyboard forces the students to think about picture composition, camera angles, locations, and props.

Storyboarding is most helpful for scripted productions, such as a commercial or a movie. Storyboards are not as helpful for videos that capture live action, such as a news broadcast, game show, or documentary. Few professional directors will attempt a production without storyboarding it in detail. That way, all the major decisions are made before the cameras are turned on, and oversights that delay production are avoided. In the advertising industry, storyboards are invaluable in communicating design concepts to the customer for approval before the expense of production is incurred.

For their productions, I supply my students with storyboard templates (figure 4.2 will be filled out) to allow them to map their productions. I use stick figures to show students that the point is not to make each frame a work of art but rather a symbolic representation of major elements in the picture.

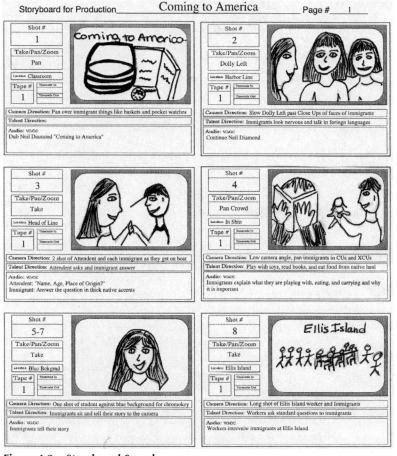

Figure 4.2   Storyboard Sample

The storyboard template I have students use allows for much of the work of scripting to be accomplished on the storyboard as well (figure 4.2). Each frame of the storyboard has the following:

- Viewfinder—in which you draw the image of the scene
- Shot Number—for sequencing the shots
- Type of Shot—take, pan, or zoom
- Location—where the shot will take place
- Tape Number—to record which tape was used to film the shot, with timecodes, in and out, to locate the shot on the tape
- Camera Direction—to let the camera operator know what to do
- Talent Direction—to let the talent know what to do
- Audio—where the voice-over (VO) or on camera (OC) text is placed for each scene.

Computer programs exist to assist students in creating more professional-looking storyboards by providing a drawing program with clipart that can be rotated and resized. One such program is StoryBoard Quick by Power Productions, www.powerproduction.com (figure 4.3). The program is $280 with a limited offering of clipart, and additional clipart packages are $50 per package.

Figure 4.3 Storyboard Quick by Power Productions

Storyboard Quick allows you to create storyboards using clipart of people and objects that can be rotated, resized, and placed in various settings.

SHOT LISTS

For those productions that cannot be scripted and storyboarded easily, a shot list may be more useful (figure 4.4). If students planning a production want to include important shots, I have them complete a shot list. On this form the students list what shots they need and associated talent, props, and equipment. The checkbox to the left allows them to check off the shots as they capture them.

This form is helpful for students who want to produce a video on something like a Halloween fair. For such an event, the students would not be able to storyboard the production because they could not know exactly what was going to happen and when. A shot list would allow them to think

Shot List

Production: Coming to America _____

❑ Shot Immigrants standing in line _____ Location Back of Class _____

   Talent Everyone _____ Props _____ Equipment_____

❑ Shot Getting on boat _____ Location Front of Class _____

   Talent Everyone _____ Props Hat for Attendent Equipment_____

❑ Shot Picture of the Statue of Liberty _____ Location Off the Internet ___

   Talent_____ Props_____ Equipment_____

❑ Shot Picture of the Statue of Liberty _____ Location Off the Internet ___

   Talent_____ Props_____ Equipment_____

❑ Shot Picture of the Flag _____ Location Off CD Rom _____

   Talent_____ Props_____ Equipment_____

Figure 4.4   Shot List Example

A shot list is another way your students can plan and organize their productions.

ahead about the shots they would want to include in the production. They would list such things as "students in costume next to the fair's poster," "students setting up for the fair," "Kindergarten teacher telling class about the fair and students' excited reaction," "going into the haunted house," or "Mrs. Bannard in her costume." By filling in the lines for talent, props, and special equipment, the students think about the needs for each shot. They will be prepared with a light for the haunted house, and will find students in costume to stand next to the poster.

RELEASE FORMS

If a production has the potential of reaching a wide audience, such as local TV or distribution to other schools, it would be a good idea to secure release forms from those individuals (or their guardians if they are under 18) whose images are used. If your students are shooting in a public place such as a playground, it could be enough for them to let everyone know what they are doing and assume that if people stay they are consenting to allow their images to be used. A sample release form is in the appendix.

If your students hope to shoot footage on private property, it will be important for them to obtain permission from the owner of the property. This should be taken care of in the preproduction phase so that alternate plans can be made if necessary.

CONCLUSION

Preproduction is the most important phase in the production process. Take care to impress upon the students the importance of planning their production, and require them to fill out whatever forms you think they will need to formalize the preproduction process. The more work they do in this phase of production, the better. Students will inevitably want to spend little time in this phase and move right into production, where they perceive their time best spent. However, without the proper planning, they could waste time shooting and editing footage that is inconsistent and incomplete, and ultimately produce a video that is ineffective.

Chapter Five

Production

The production phase is when the actual shooting takes place, and the students will capture the action in front of the camera. In this chapter, the basics of using a digital video camera to capture footage will be covered as well as elementary lighting and sound principles. Unfortunately, the reality of what is happening in front of the camera will not just jump onto the tape. Simply pointing the camera at the action without forethought or variation will produce, at best, an uninteresting video. Your students will also have to learn the many limitations of the camera. The camera is not as adept as the human eye at compensating for different lighting, nor is it able to focus as deeply or quickly. The camera's lens, which is not as wide as our vision, allows the camera to see only a narrow sliver of what is in front of it. The audio recording available through the built-in microphone is also inferior to our own sense of hearing and will be compromised by wind, background noise, or even the sound of the camera's motor turning the tape. These limitations of the camera can prevent it from capturing usable footage in low light and soft sound situations. Your students will have to learn what is an unacceptable condition for the camera and understand that just because they are able to see and hear everything that is happening on the set does not mean the camera can capture it.

To help your students recreate the realistic feel of a video shoot, this chapter will also discuss camera movements, various shots, and crew positions, and will identify terms relating to these aspects of production. When planning and executing a production, the students should use industry standard names and abbreviations for each of the camera movements and different shots so that the writer, director, and camera operator all understand where the camera should be and the way in which the camera should move.

Each position of the crew is delineated so that your students can assume the many roles and divide the many responsibilities among themselves. In addition, the jargon of the trade, the sequence of action, and director's cues are outlined for a typical video shoot so that your students can adopt the language used by professionals.

CAMERA BASICS

Every digital video camera can be set in at least three modes: camera, VCR (or VTR), and off (figure 5.1). The camera mode is used to record video and sound from the lens and microphone. The VCR (sometime VTR for video tape recorder) mode turns the camera into a miniDV VCR, allowing you to replay footage from a miniDV tape. The off mode turns the camera off and recharges the batteries if it is plugged into the wall.

A forth mode, called memory or still image, exists on some cameras. This allows the camera to take still images and save them onto a removable medium like a Memory Stick (Sony), MultiMediaCard^t (Canon and others) or Secure Digital (SD) Media Card (Panasonic and others). In this mode, the digital video camcorder acts like a digital camera. Once images

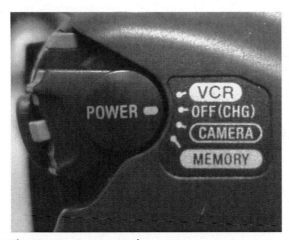

Figure 5.1　Camera Modes

Every digital video camera is equipped with at least three modes; Camera, VCR (or VTR), and Off. If it has the ability to take still images and save them to a removable media device, it will have another mode, memory.

are captured on these cards or sticks, you will need to use an adapter connected to the computer that can read the cards and import the images to its hard drive. Some of the newer cameras now come with a USB port that allows you to plug the camera directly into the computer, avoiding the need for an adapter.

To record video, you need only load the digital video camera with miniDV tape, remove the lens cap, switch the camera into camera mode, and hit the red button at your thumb. Through the viewfinder or on the LCD panel you will see a red "Rec" or "Record." Hitting the red button again will stop the recording. That is all you need to know to capture footage using a digital video camcorder. However, Dr. John Bunch, professor of video production at University of Virginia, likens shooting video to shooting a gun—while simply pulling the trigger makes one a shooter, it takes skill beyond the basics to be a marksmen. So too in video, anyone can point a camera and capture video, but it takes skill to capture video that is clear, interesting, and compelling.

The few simple instructions below will allow your students to differentiate their videos from 95 percent of all other home videos and create professional-looking presentations.

THE THREE Ss—STRAIGHT, STEADY, AND SMOOTH

At minimum you want to teach your students the three Ss of video, shoot Straight, Steady, and Smooth (York 2001, 68). The use of a tripod will go a long way in helping students capture video that adheres to the three Ss. To keep the video straight, the camera should be level so that the horizon is not skewed and the actors tipped over. To make the video steady, the camera should be mounted on a tripod, braced against something solid, or at the very least held with both hands—one of which should be underneath the camera. To make the video footage smooth, the camera should be moved using fluid movements.

Students should use a tripod whenever possible to make the resulting video dramatically better than handheld video. When purchasing a tripod, make sure that it has a fluid head, which provides smooth action when panning or tilting; a ball-level, which tells you if the camera is level; and a quick release plate, which allows you to remove the camera from and reattach it to the tripod quickly. The Velbon Videomate is an excellent choice, as it has all of these features at a reasonable price.

If the camera has to move during shooting, a dolly is very useful. This device has wheels and attaches to the bottom of a tripod, allowing it to roll around a flat surface smoothly. Wheelchairs and shopping carts are other favorites of low budget filmmakers for moving the camera to capture action.

Another option is to turn on the image stabilization feature now available in almost every model of digital video camera. This feature attempts to reduce the bumps and jumps caused by handheld movement; however, it does consume more battery power.

LIGHTING

As Barry Hampe (1997), the author and videographer, says, a video "is made with light." The camera requires light to bounce off the subject to create an image that is recordable. Too much light and the picture will wash out with white blotches, causing figures and colors to become faint or indistinguishable. Too little light and the picture becomes dark and equally unusable. The amount of light used and its relationship to the subject are critical to the camera's ability to represent figures and colors accurately.

Exposure

The amount of light will determine the exposure, with too much causing overexposure and too little causing underexposure. Overexposed footage is too bright and washes out color and has hot spots that are all white. Too much light from a single source, such as direct sunlight on a cloudless day, causes not only hot spots but also dark shadows. There are two easy ways to correct this problem: one, take cover in the shade of a tree or building; or, two, use a reflector to bounce light back onto the subject to even out the brightness of the subject and lessen the deep shadows (figure 5.2). The reflectors need not be expensive professional grade. Inexpensive windshield sun blockers work well and fold up for easy storage. Some windshield blockers have a shiny reflective side and

Figure 5.2   Using Reflectors

Too much light from a single source, such as direct sunlight, causes dark shadows. There are two easy ways to correct this problem; use a reflector to reflect light back on the subject or shade the subject. The reflector will bounce light into shadows. Shading the subject will even the lighting and soften the lines.

a white side, giving your students two different reflective surfaces with which to work.

For low light situations, extra lights may be required. Here again, inexpensive clip-on lamps work well for adding extra light to a set. Different wattage bulbs can be used to vary the amount of light added. Professionals use a three point lighting configuration that is composed of a key light, a fill light, and a backlight (figure 5.3). The key light provides most of the light and illuminates the subject. The fill light takes away some of the deep shadows but leaves enough shadow in place to define the features of

All Three Lights

Spot Light   Fill Light

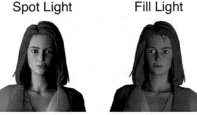

Back Light

Figure 5.3   Three Point Lighting

Three point lighting configuration that is composed of key light, a fill light, and a backlight. Each contributes to correctly lighting a subject. The Spot Light provides the primary light and shadows. The Fill Light fills in some of the hard shadows created by the Spot Light. The Back Light gives the subject some depth and separates it from the background.

the subject. The backlight separates the subject from its environment by creating a thin line of light around the subject and adds to the sculpting of the subject.

Backlighting

The most common mistake made by students when lighting a subject is placing the subject in front of a bright background. This causes the camera to darken the entire picture to compensate for the bright background, causing all definition of the subject to be lost in a dark silhouette (figure 5.4). To avoid this situation, encourage your students to place their subjects against darker backgrounds.

It is sometimes very difficult to judge the amount of key light and background light needed, because the LCD screen on the camera will show much more definition of the subject than is actually being recorded. Experience and reshooting are the best bets to get the right amount of light in a shot.

Figure 5.4   Backlighting

Bright backgrounds can cause a dark figure.

Color

Light actually has a color, called color temperature. You may notice that when you walk into a gymnasium lit by mercury lights, everything initially appear yellowish; or when you walk into a room lit by florescent lights, things appear steely blue or green depending on the tube. The human eye and mind adjust to these different lighting situations and quickly compensate for the different lighting colors. The camera also tries to adjust for different colors of light using its "white balance." All digital video cameras have an automatic white balance, which tries to figure out what is white. Once it knows what is supposed to be white in a given lighting situation, it can adjust to represent all of the other colors more accurately. Most digital video cameras allow you to override the automatic white balance and choose from a set of preset white balance options.

The more expensive cameras have a manual white balance feature that sets the camera's white balance in any lighting situation. To use this feature, just before shooting, zoom into something pure white, like a clean sheet of paper, so that it fills the entire screen, then hit the white balance button. That sets the white balance and you are ready to shoot under those lighting conditions. You will need to reset the white balance for the next lighting condition.

AUDIO

In addition to the shaky camera, poor audio is the other indicator of an amateur production. To achieve professional-quality sound, you really do need professional equipment and years of training and practice. Your students will not have the equipment or time to devote to the sound aspect of their productions. However, there are some things that they can do to improve the sound of their videos.

If your students will be relying on the built-in microphone to capture the audio, they should position the camera as close to the action as they can while still getting the image they want. These microphones are convenient but are the least desirable recording devices. Canon and Sony sell clip-on shotgun mikes that attach to the hot shoe, a connection plate on the top of the camera. These microphones are better at picking up sound at a

distance than the built-in mikes and yet maintain the convenience of being attached to the camera.

The best way to improve the audio, however, is to "mike the source,"
meaning the students should use an external microphone positioned close
to the action to capture the audio. Almost all cameras have a microphone
port, allowing the students to use an external microphone.

Choosing the right type of microphone for each situation will further
improve the audio quality of the production. For specifics on the types of
microphones available and when to use them, see the microphones section
of chapter 8.

FOCUS

The automatic focus that comes with every camera will keep the closest object in the center of the frame in focus. This is fine for most of what your students will be doing. However, if they want to compose the image with the
subject off to the side in accordance with the Rule of Thirds, as discussed in
chapter 3, they will need to use the manual focus so that the camera does not
focus on the background in the center, leaving your subject out of focus.
They will also need to use the manual focus if there is something between
the subject and the camera, such as a screen door or branch. In this case, the
auto focus will focus on the closest object—the screen or branch—and leave
the subject out of focus in the background. By using the manual focus, the
students will be able to focus through or past the offending object.

A useful trick for manually focusing on a subject is to zoom way into
the subject, focus the camera, and then zoom back out. It is easier to gauge
the focus when the camera is tight on the subject and the subject consumes
the entire viewfinder. When you zoom back out, the picture will stay in
perfect focus. This is an especially useful trick if the shot involves a zoom,
because the camera will already be in focus.

ZOOMING

Interestingly, amateurs love to zoom in and out of shots, which gives them
a sense of power and control. For that reason, manufacturers place the

zoom rocker right under the fingers of the camera operator for easy access. However, professionals almost never use a zoom. Zooms are an unnatural way to enlarge the subject, and you should encourage your students to use the zoom as little as possible.

If the students want to get a closer shot of something, encourage them to move the camera closer. In moving close to the subject, the subject alone will get bigger; with a zoom the subject and background will increase in size together.

An alternative to a zoom is a series of incrementally closer shots that fade into each other. To achieve this, start with a wide shot, zoom in and hold the image; and then, when editing the video, cut out the zooming portions and replace them with a fade. This technique for getting closer to a subject is more dramatic and less distracting than a zoom.

The few zooms that are used in profession videos are: a very slow zoom into a subject as the scene gets more personal, and those zooms used for special effects. A special effect could be used to capture someone coming to a sudden realization, or to shift quickly to a specific object that has become the focus of the scene.

FRAMING THE SHOT

The camera operator will want to compose the images of the video using the principles discussed in chapter 3. The biggest mistake student camera operators make is looking *through* the LCD panel or viewfinder at what is going on in the shot as if looking through a window. The camera operator should be looking *at* the LCD panel or viewfinder as a picture and concentrating on framing the subjects. If the camera operator is watching the faces of the actors and watching the action *through* the viewfinder, then he or she is not concentrating on the composition of the shot.

Professional camera operators train themselves to survey the entire picture, look at the edges of the shot, and treat the subjects as silhouettes to make sure that the subjects are correctly positioned in the shot. The saying goes, "Take care of the edges [of the picture] and the shot will take care of itself."

The camera operator also has to be thinking ahead to what is going to happen, so that the camera is proactive in anticipating the action, and have the camera in the right place, rather than constantly reacting to movement and chasing the action around.

EXTRA FOOTAGE BEFORE AND AFTER EACH SCENE

Another simple rule of thumb to follow is to get extra footage before and after each shot. When the students edit the video, the extra footage will allow them to fade into or out of the scene or cross dissolve one clip with another. Fades and cross dissolves need a second or two of footage that does not contain important action or audio. The director will have to coach the actors to hold their positions for three to five seconds before and after each take to create this extra footage.

POWER CORD VS. BATTERY

When at all possible, the students should plug the camera into the wall and use the power cord for the camera. That way they save the battery for when they need it and do not unnecessarily tax the battery, which does degrade with use.

When wall plugs are not available and extended shooting is necessary, students should be equipped with spare batteries. If battery power is still an issue, there are ways to conserve battery power.

Ways to conserve the battery are as follows:

• Turn the camera off between shots.
• Use the viewfinder instead of the LCD panel.
• Turn off the image stabilization feature.
• Do not use external devices powered by the camera.
• Turn the camera off between takes.

EXTENDED PLAY—DO NOT USE

Many digital cameras now have extended play capability that allows you to capture more than 60 minutes on a single miniDV tape. Do NOT use extended play for capturing footage. Since extended play is incompatible with most digital video editors, your students will not be able to export extended play footage to the computer for editing. They will have to export the footage to another tape or format to import it into the video editor.

CAMERA SPECIAL EFFECTS

Most digital video cameras have the ability to impose special effects on the video footage while you capture it. Discourage your students from ever using the effects built into the camera. It is better to capture the footage on the camera at its highest quality and impose any effects in postproduction in a "nondestructive editing" environment using the video editing software. Using the software, students can add the same effects; and if they do not like an effect, it can be removed and the original footage restored. If you employ the effect in the camera, you will have applied those effects in a destructive editing environment. There will be no way to undo the effect because the camera will have recorded the images with the effect indelibly woven into the footage.

CAMERA MOVEMENT

Each camera movement has a name and abbreviation that are used when scripting and producing a video (figure 5.5).

Figure 5.5   Camera Movements

- Dolly In and Out (DI, DO)—Move the whole camera in and out. To create the smoothest dolly shots, use a tripod with a dolly, a wheelchair, a shopping cart, or some other wheeled cart to move the camera around.
- Truck Left and Right (TL, TR)—Move the whole camera left and right. Again this works best if the camera is mounted on some rolling device.
- Arc Left and Right (AL, AR)—Move the whole camera in an arc as if the camera were tethered to the subject by a string.
- Pedestal Up and Down (PU, PD)—Move the whole camera higher and lower. Most tripods have a hand crank that can raise or lower the camera to some degree. Additional adjustment for a tripod comes from adjusting the length of the legs.
- Zoom In and Out (ZI, ZO)—Use the zoom on the camera to get closer or further away. This method of getting closer to the subject has the unnatural effect of magnifying the background as well as the subject. Zooms are best conducted slowly, so as to not draw attention to themselves, or saved for special effects. Some cameras have a zoom ring, which allows greater control than the zoom rockers offered on most cameras.
- Pan Left and Right (PL, PR)—Pivot the camera horizontally left and right. This shot is like turning your head left and right. When panning a panorama, it is best done from left to right, as this is the most natural viewing pattern to our culture, which reads left to right.
- Tilt Up and Down (TU, TD)—Pivot camera vertically up and down. This shot is like looking up and down.

180 DEGREE RULE

When taping an event, such as a conversation between two people or a sporting event, it is important to identify the axis of action, the direction in which the action is taking place (figure 5.6). For a conversation between two people, the line would be drawn so that it connected to the two people. For a sporting event, such as a soccer game, the line would be drawn connecting the two goals. In most cases, the axis of action will be drawn in the direction that people are facing. The action takes place back and forth along this line.

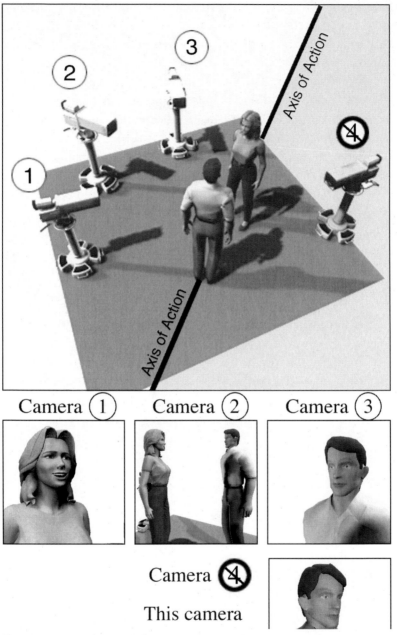

Camera ①   Camera ②   Camera ③

Camera ④

This camera

Figure 5.6   180 Degree Rule

The 180 degree states that all cameras should not cross the axis of action. To do so disorients the viewer by having the subjects no longer face each other.

This axis of action should act as an imaginary line that the camera should not cross when going from one shot to another (figure 5.6). If the camera crosses the line, it is very disorienting to the viewer. Imagine a video composed of shots between the cameras on the correct side of the line in figure 5.6. You could imagine a conversation that would go from the woman (camera 1) to the two of them (camera 2) to the man (camera 3) and back and forth. The positioning of the cameras on only one side of the axis of action makes it clear that they are looking at each other. If you introduce the image of the man from a camera that has crossed the line (camera 4), he would be oriented so that he was looking the same direction as the woman and not turned toward her in conversation. This would be confusing to the viewer, who would expect the man to be looking right toward the woman. The camera that crosses the line also is in a position that captures camera 1 in the background.

PRODUCTION SHOTS

Various camera shots are used in production to change the perspective of the camera and to capture action in varying degrees of detail. The following are the most commonly used shots and their respective purposes. Share with your students the different shots and encourage them to use a variety of techniques to enhance their productions.

A-Roll and B-Roll

A-roll is a term for footage that is primary to the video. In a newscast the A-roll footage would be of the anchorperson or reporter talking to the camera or interviewing a person. This footage carries the story and provides the important information.

B-roll refers to the footage that is spliced into the A-roll footage to provide extra visual context to the story or relevant images. For example, a story about new athletic fields might be filmed as a conversation between a student reporter and the athletic director. The A-roll would be the conversation, but when the athletic director began to talk about the land that will be developed for the new fields, the B-roll would be a pan of the undeveloped property. This would be spliced into the final video to complement the A-roll footage.

Some videographers turn this concept on its head and consider the B-roll to be the most important aspect of a video. They prefer to have the images that would be considered B-roll carry the story. They attempt to create a compelling story through imagery rather than tell the story through words.

One Shot

A one shot has one person in it.

Two Shot

A two shot has two people in it.

Group Shot

A group shot features a group of people.

Primary and Reverse Angle Shot

The primary shot is the shot that is most important to the story in a given scene. In an interview, the primary shot would be of the interviewee. In a drama, it would be of the principle actor.

The reverse angle shot is the complement to the primary shot in which the camera flashes back to the interviewer or the secondary actor. When setting up for the reverse angle shot, be sure to line up the actors' eyes so that they are looking at each other.

In an interview using a single camera, the reverse angle shots of the interviewer have to be videotaped after the interview is over. The interviewer has an obligation to re-ask the questions verbatim. It is best if the students prepare a list of questions ahead of time and read from the list to ensure the accuracy of re-asked questions. Ad-libbed questions should be written down during the interview so that they can be re-asked with accuracy. The students can also refer to the taped interview to get the precise wording of the questions. In the editing phase, the re-asked questions and answers can be pieced together, making it appear as though there were two cameras in the interview.

Figure 5.7   Over-the-Shoulder Shot

Over-the-Shoulder Shot

This shot views a subject over the shoulder of another person (figure 5.7). This is an interesting way to compose a shot with two people. The person's shoulder adds depth to the picture, and the viewer enjoys a frontal view of the person in conversation.

Reaction Shots

Reaction shots are close-ups of a person reacting to something that is happening, a comment, or a question that is being asked.

Establishing Shots

An extreme long shot or long shot is used to establish the surroundings of the subject and contextualize the subsequent action.

Dolly Shot

In a dolly shot the camera is mounted on a dolly, then rolled along to follow the action.

Matte Shot

Mattes are cutouts that are placed in front of the lens and used to frame the action. A popular matte is a heart shaped cutout used to frame two people in love.

THE VIDEO CREW

Video is best produced in a collaborative environment. Members of the crew have responsibilities as outlined by their job description. Your students should be divided into the various positions, with many filling multiple roles.

Producer

The producer is ultimately responsible for the entire production. It is this person's job to make sure that everyone and everything comes together for the production to happen. The producer will, in many cases, oversee the writing of the script.

If you assign a video project with a specific topic and treatment, in many ways you are acting as the producer. How involved you get in overseeing the production after you have assigned the project is up to you. Some producers are present at every production session and micromanage the production, while others leave all production details and responsibilities to the director.

If the students are required to create a topic and treatment and then pitch their idea to you for approval, they are acting as the producers, with you being a network or studio executive.

Producers are also known as suits in the industry because they are frequently businesspeople concerned with the economics and viability of a production. Their concern is making sure the production is completed on time and on budget.

Director

The director is in charge during the production and postproduction of a video, turning the script and vision into a video. The director makes the artistic decisions during the production and directs the efforts of the video crew and talent. The director is also responsible for the logistics of a production, making sure that the production stays on schedule and is finished on time. Once the shooting is completed, the director oversees the postproduction phase, when the video is edited and polished for distribution.

Directors, while they are in charge of the production, are frequently more artistic and less businesslike. They frequently miss scheduled deadlines and go over budget. Let's hope your students do not too closely approximate all the characteristics of the director.

Scriptwriter

The scriptwriter writes the script and might prepare storyboards and a shot list.

Talent

Talent refers to the cast of a production. Within the talent category, there are two groups: performers, who act as hosts or reporters, and actors, who play theatrical roles. Performers are sometimes referred to as hairdos. Extras constitute another category and are the individuals who appear in a video but have no speaking roles.

Camera Operator

The camera operator is responsible for operating the camera, framing the shot, and taping the footage. This person should be thoroughly familiar with the operation of the camera and have a good sense of video aesthetics.

In student video productions, the camera is also the device used to capture the audio, so the camera operators must also concern themselves with the recording of the audio. They should be sure to have the camera close enough to the action for the camera to record the audio or be sure to mike the source. In the professional world, this would be the domain of the audio operator.

The camera operator will also be responsible for making sure that the scene is properly lit. This could involve using extra lights or repositioning the actors in a more suitable lighting condition. The camera operator should also be careful not to shoot figures against an overly bright background. In the professional world, this would be the domain of a lighting director.

To help in postproduction, it is useful for the camera operator to make sure each take is slated. For the first few seconds of each take, a piece of paper or clapstick (a board with a clapper on the top that snaps when closed) with the name of the production, scene, and take is held up to the camera. The slate helps identify the takes and keeps them straight when the footage is imported into the editing software. This job is normally the responsibility of a production assistant; in student productions anyone who is not otherwise busy should man the slate.

As you can see, being a camera operator in a single-camera student production is a huge responsibility.

Editor

The editor is responsible for piecing together the captured footage in the postproduction phase of the video. This person imports the video into the computer and manipulates the editing software to assemble the raw footage into a polished finished product. Frequently, this person will take directions from the director, but sometimes the editor will be given license to make all the artistic decisions to assemble a pleasing final product.

Graphics Operator

A graphics operator generates the graphics and titles for a video. Since most of this work is now done on the computer, this person may have responsibility for the opening scene or closing credits to a video. The graphics operator might also generate any static images that are required for a production, such as a chart or page of text.

Grip

A grip is a union-defined position for someone responsible for carrying equipment, setting up lights and cameras, and running all the cables. In most student productions, all participants can add this title to their list.

Other Positions

Other positions that a student production might require are propmasters, makeup artists, set builders, costume designers, and choreographers.

DIRECTOR'S CUES

During production, the director should use a series of standard calls and set procedures to direct the efforts of the video crew. A consistency of protocol allows the crew to anticipate their responsibilities by following standard operating procedures with clearly defined and universally understood jargon.

Be sure that the directors of the student productions are familiar with these protocols and jargon, and encourage them to adopt these procedures. The students have seen the procedures and jargon many times in movies and on TV, and will find it thrilling to be part of the action.

Here are the procedures and director's cues for a typical scene:

- Director: "Places everybody"—Everyone gets into place.
- Director: "Quiet on the set"—Everyone quiets down.
- Director: "Standby camera, standby talent"—The camera and talent should be ready.
- Camera operator: Holds slate or clapstick up to camera
- Director: "Roll tape"—The camera operator hits the record button and begins taping.
- Camera operator: Takes slate or clapstick away after two or three seconds and focuses on subject(s)
- Camera operator: Gives a nod when picture is framed and in focus, and tape is rolling
- Director: Watches the camera operator to see when the nod is given to signify that everything is in focus and the tape is rolling

- Director: Waits seven to nine seconds from when tape began rolling
- Director: "Action"—This begins the scene but does not necessarily mean that actors should start speaking their parts right away. If the actors delay their lines by even a few seconds, it will make editing easier by giving the editor a little footage with which to work transitions and fades. The director might even give another nonverbal cue, such as pointing to the actors, to indicate that they should start their lines.
- Actors: Wait until they are given the sign to act and then begin the scene
- Scene takes place
- Scene ends
- Director: Waits three to five seconds—At the end of the scene, the actors should pause in their places, again allowing for extra footage at the end of the scene with which to work transitions and fades during editing.
- Director: "Cut"—The scene is over. The camera operator stops taping. Everyone relaxes.

CONCLUSION

There is no substitute for experience when working in the production phase. It takes experience and experimentation to understand what amount of light is needed or how close the microphone should be to the source. For these reasons, initial student productions should be small in scale and based locally, so that reshooting footage is an option. Through the process of shooting and reshooting, the students will become quite expert at capturing the footage they want and making the video of their design a reality.

If the preproduction phase has been done properly, the production phase is sometimes the shortest of the three phases. It is an exciting phase, one that the students look forward to and greatly enjoy.

Once the footage is captured, it is on to the final phase, postproduction!

Chapter Six

Postproduction

After you have captured footage, you are ready to edit and distribute the video. These two events take place in postproduction, or simply "post." At a basic level, the footage will be moved from the camera to the computer using a nonlinear editing software of your choice and a Firewire connection (IEEE 1394 or iLink). The footage is manipulated in the editing program, and transitions, titles, music, and voice-overs are added using a nonlinear editing program (NLE).

Which nonlinear editing program you choose will depend in part on your preference for the Mac or PC platform. An overview of available equipment for both platforms follows. Minimanuals for Apple's iMovie 2 for Mac and an overview of Pinnacle Studio versions 7 and 8 for Windows are contained within this chapter.

COMPUTER HARDWARE FOR DIGITAL VIDEO EDITING

System Requirements

In terms of systems requirements, digital video is the most demanding consumer application. A computer expected to handle digital video has to be able to import large amounts of data from the camera, have hard drives big enough to store the captured video, be fast enough to keep up with the import, and have a processor fast enough to render the video effects and transitions in a reasonable amount of time. Fortunately, this is no longer an expensive high-end computer. Most low-end computers now come with hard drives big enough and processors fast enough to handle video.

Thanks to the accuracy of Moore's Law, which predicts that computers will double in complexity every year to 18 months, computers have reached the point at which digital video is possible on every Macintosh and many of the PCs you can purchase today.

Every computer handling video will have to have Firewire or IEEE 1394 connectors. These allow you to connect the digital video camera to the computer, to move the footage from the camera to the computer, and then, once edited, to move the finished video back to the camera. This technology was developed by Apple but was made a standard by the Institute of Electrical and Electronics Engineers (IEEE), and is used by all major manufacturers of computers, digital video cameras, and peripherals such as hard drives, CD and DVD burners, and scanners. Sony prefers to use the name iLink to avoid paying royalties on the name Firewire. Firewire has been standard on all Macintosh computers since 1999. It does not come standard on most PCs, and it may be necessary to add this hardware to your Windows computers. Adding a Firewire card to a PC costs around $50.

Hard drive space is at a premium for digital video editing. The more hard drive space you have available, the more projects you can have going at the same time. Each minute of digital video takes approximately 230 MB of hard drive space. Student projects are normally about 5 to 15 minutes long, but students usually capture about twice as much video as they need, meaning they import 10 to 30 minutes of video per project. If they save their project as a file so that they can burn the video to a DVD disk, they will use another 5 to 15 minutes of video. Totaled and calculated in hard disk space, each project will consume somewhere between 3.5 and 10 GB, depending on the length of the video and how much extra footage the groups import. When you take into consideration that about 4 GB of each hard drive is taken up by the operating system of the computer, programs, and data, a 20-GB hard drive (about as small as they come now) can support 1 to 3 projects, a 40-GB drive 4 to 8 projects, and a 60-GB drive 5 to 16. Obviously, when deciding how much hard drive space to buy, more is always better for working with video. Smaller drives will require that you be vigilant about clearing finished projects to make room for new ones. Larger drives will enable you to be more relaxed about moving projects off the system once they are completed and will allow for larger projects.

You will also have to make sure that the speed of the hard disk is fast enough to sustain the read and write throughput to support digital video. All Macintosh computer hard drives made since 1999 support digital video capture and output. On the PC side, the preferred drive is a SCSI drive (pronounced "scuzzy"), which will ensure necessary hard disk speeds. Other disk options may not be fast enough. When buying external drives, make sure that they operate at 7,200 rpm (revolutions per minute) or higher. The more rpms, the faster the access speed.

The speed of the computer's processor will play an important part when you employ any special effects or transitions. In these cases, the computer will have to render the effects, which will require the computer to calculate and build a rendered video, frame by frame. This can take some time and in the professional world, time is money—most professionals are willing to purchase premium equipment for the extra processor speed. I have found that the speed of the processor is not as much a factor in educational settings and that students' tolerance for delay during renderings permits the purchase of a low-end machine. Sometimes if a group has asked the computer for significant rendering to take place, they simply let the computer render while they go to lunch or let the computer render overnight. The speed of the processor is also an issue when the computer exports the video from the editing program into another format for distribution. This procedure is processor intensive, as it requires many calculations to compress the video into another format.

A DVD burner provides an effective way to export videos in a high-quality format on a durable medium that is easily stored. It is also a convenient way to make the videos available to the students, as discussed earlier in this chapter. A CD burner will enable you to make Video Compact Discs (VCDs), but the resolution in this format is noticeably inferior to that of a DVD. A CD burner with the right software will also allow you to create Super Video Compact Discs (SVCDs), which enjoy DVD quality but on a regular CD. The problem with this format is that few DVD players can read SVCDs.

Apple/Mac

Out of the box, Apple's 800 MHz flat panel iMac comes with a 60 GB hard drive, Firewire, iMovie 2, iDVD 2, and a SuperDrive that burns CDs and DVDs (DVD-RW/CD-RW, RW standing for read and write). This computer has everything you need to import, edit, and export movies to DVD in one small footprint. At present, this machine is selling for $1,800 to educational institutions.

The less-expensive iMacs are also equipped to import and edit movies, but they do not have the SuperDrive to enable them to author DVDs. They can, however, output movies to all the other distribution formats. In fact, all Macs made since 1999 are capable of importing and editing digital video. In 1999 Apple began making Firewire ports standard on all its computers. These ports allow you to connect a DV camera to the computer and move massive amounts of data from the camera to the computer. Firewire is also useful for connecting external hard drives, allowing you to store the many GBs of data required in digital video (more on expanded hard drives in chapter 9).

As Macs come with the necessary ports and editing software as standard, with one model equipped with a DVD burner, they are an excellent choice for digital video editing.

PC
Hardware

PCs do not enjoy the uniformity in hardware and software that Macs do, but they make up for this through a range of options. Most hardware manufacturers will be able to configure a computer tailored for digital video editing, but it may require a custom configuration or purchase of additional hardware to ensure that all of the necessary components are present. Required hardware includes a large hard drive (20 GB or more) and Firewire ports (IEEE 1394 or iLink). If you wish to output your movies on DVD, a DVD-RW drive will also be necessary.

Every major manufacturer of PCs produces a computer tailored for digital video with large hard drives, Firewire, and a fast processor. Amazingly enough, these computers can be purchased for well under $2,000.

Software

This hardware can be used to power a nonlinear digital video editing software package. The two predominant consumer-level digital video editing programs I recommend are iMovie 2 for the Mac and Pinnacle Studio-version 7 or 8 for Windows. A minimanual for iMovie and an overview for Studio follow. The iMovie section is more thorough because a manual is not provided, while Studio comes with a complete manual.

iMovie 2 Minimanual

iMovie 2 is an elegant video editing program from Apple. Although simple in design and interface, iMovie allows you to create very sophisticated, professional-looking videos. It takes me only 50 minutes to teach the average student how to use almost every feature in iMovie. This section will act as a minimanual, highlighting many of iMovie's capabilities. Since iMovie comes without a manual, this section will go into more depth than the next section on Pinnacle Studio version 7.

Where to Get iMovie

iMovie 2 comes free with every new Mac that has been sold since 2000 and comes free with Mac OS X. For those computers bought after 2000, iMovie is preinstalled in the applications folder of the hard drive, and an iMovie CD comes bundled with the computer. If your Mac was made before 2000 and you are not running Mac OS X, iMovie 2 can be purchased for $50 and downloaded from Apple. The upgrade from iMovie to iMovie 2 is $20 and can be downloaded from the Apple website.

Which Operating System Should You Use, Mac OS 9.x or OS X?

iMovie runs very well in both OS 9.x and OS X, and video files can be exchanged between the two operating systems. You can start a movie in the OS 9 version and then open it and continue to edit it in the OS X version. In short, if you have not made the switch to OS X, iMovie is not going to provide you with a reason to make the move.

What Computer Will Run iMovie 2?

iMovie will run on any Mac with OS 8.5 or better, but the installer will object to installing it on operating systems below 9.1. To take full advantage of iMovie, you will need a computer with a Firewire connection to transfer the video footage to and from the DV camera. However, for the purposes of teaching my students how to use iMovie's editing features, I am able to use a lab of older iMacs that do not have Firewire but do have iMovie and the tutorial file, which contains 45 seconds of prerecorded footage. In the lab, I run the tutorial with my students to acquaint them with the program; and then, when they are ready to work on their projects, I move them in groups to the few newer iMacs that have the Firewire ports and larger hard drives.

Large hard drive capacity is not required to run iMovie, but it is a practical necessity when working with digital video. Using about 230 megabytes (MB) of hard drive space per minute of video, an average student project will range in size from 3.5 to 10 GB. A Mac with Firewire ports can expand its storage capacity with Firewire hard drives relatively easily (see chapter 9).

Launch iMovie 2

iMovie 2 can be found in the applications folder on the hard drive on the computer. Simply click on the iMovie 2 icon in OS X or open the iMovie 2 folder and double click on the iMovie 2 icon in OS 9.x (figure 6.1). When you start iMovie 2 a splash screen will prompt you to open the existing project, create a new project, or quit the program.

Figure 6.1   iMovie Program Locations

iMovie is located in the Applications Folder in both OS 9.x and OS X.

Meet iMovie

The iMovie interface consumes the entire screen and divides the desktop into three areas: the monitor, the shelf, and the timeline (figure 6.2). The monitor allows you to preview video footage from the camera, clips from the shelf or timeline, or sequenced clips in the form of a video from the timeline. The shelf is where clips are stored as they are captured from the camera. The buttons on the bottom of the shelf access the transition panel, where you can add transitions between clips in the timeline; the titles panels, where you can add text to the video; the effects panel, where you can change the look of segments by adding special effects; and the audio panel, where you can add voice-overs and music scores to the video. The timeline below allows you to sequence the clip in an icon or timeline view.

Figure 6.2   iMovie Interface

iMovie is divided into three areas: the Monitor, the Shelf, and the Timeline View. The Monitor allows you to view and import video from the digital video camera, and view clips on the shelf or the edited video from the timeline. The Shelf displays the clips as well and provides the panels to add transitions, titles, special effects, and audio tracks. The Timeline can be viewed in the Clip View or the Timeline View.

Importing Digital Video into iMovie

Connecting the Digital Video Camera
to the Computer

Firewire cables allow you to connect your computer and digital camera. There are only two pin-outs for Firewire, four pin and six pin. Macintosh computers have a six-pin port and digital video cameras have a four-pin port, making the cable that connects them a four-to-six-pin Firewire cable. A 14-foot four-to-six-pin cable makes conducting the class exercise described in chapter 3 much easier, allowing you to move about with the camera still connected to the computer (figure 6.3).

Once it is connected, load the camera with the tape you want to edit and turn it on to VTR or VCR mode. In this mode, your camera will act like a tape playback device and play the footage into the computer in real time. Unfortunately, there is no way to import the video from tape faster than real time. If you have 20 minutes of footage to import, it will take 20 minutes to play it into the computer for capture.

However, you can record footage directly to your hard drive by switching your camera over to camera mode while it is connected to the computer. This is how you would connect the camera to the computer for the class exercise in chapter 3. In this way, you could demonstrate for the

Figure 6.3   Connecting the DV Camera to the Computer

Use a Firewire cable to connect the digital video camera to the computer's Firewire port. Use a 6 pin to 4 pin cable as shown in the illustration. Switch the camera to VTR and iMovie to camera mode in the lower left of the Monitor window.

class the different aesthetic techniques by capturing the footage directly to the hard drive for manipulation, replay, and discussion.

It could not be simpler to connect and capture footage. There is no need to configure iMovie or load drivers for the different cameras. It really is as easy as booting iMovie, plugging in the camera, and turning it on. iMovie wakes up, recognizes there is a camera attached, and allows you to import from tape or capture in real time from the camera for editing.

For smooth capture from the camera, you must make sure that your drives have ample space for the captures and that they are defragmented. Fragmentation of the drive occurs over time when files are saved and deleted on a hard drive. The deletion of files opens a space for new files to fill. After a while, the physical spaces available for files to be saved are spread throughout the disk. When digital video is being saved to a fragmented drive, it must jump around the disk and save little pieces of the movie here and there. This sometimes causes the computer to abort a capture and complain about frames being dropped, or worse yet, freeze. To avoid this problem, you will want to run an optimizer program on your computer periodically. These programs defragment the hard drive by compacting fragments of files so that newly saved files do not have to jump around the disk looking for free spaces. Disk Warrior by Alsoft and Norton Utilities are two programs I recommend that can optimize your hard drives (see chapter 7 for more information). Optimize them after each major video project has been completed and before the next one. Since optimizing a large drive can take some time, it is not a bad idea to start your optimizations at the end of the day to be completed overnight.

Importing Video from MiniDV
Tape to iMovie

On the lower left side of the monitor is a toggle that allows you to switch from edit to camera mode (figure 6.4). In camera mode, with the camera connected and turned on to VTR, the iMovie monitor controls and displays the connected digital video camera. The fast forward, rewind, and play buttons in the monitor will fast forward, rewind, and play the tape in the camera. The big import button will capture the footage being played on the camera to the hard drive. The footage will appear in clips on the shelf to the right.

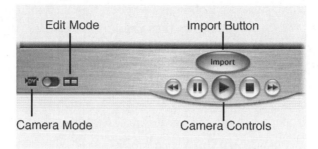

Figure 6.4   Camera and Edit Mode on Monitor

**In the lower left side of the Monitor you will find the tog-
gle for Camera Mode and Edit Mode. Switching to Camera
Mode will allow you to control the digital video camera
connected by the Firewire Cable. When in Camera Mode,
use the Camera Controls to manage the camera, and use
the Import Button to capture footage from tape. Toggle
back to Edit Mode to work with the captured clips on the
shelf or in the timeline.**

A very handy feature of iMovie is its ability to detect breaks in the footage
caused when the camera is stopped and restarted; iMovie correspondingly
saves each clip from the camera individually as a clip on the shelf. This saves
you the time and trouble of having to import one large video file and then
break it up into smaller clips prior to editing and sequencing.

Importing Video Directly from a Digital Video Camera to iMovie

If you are in camera mode in iMovie with the camera also in camera mode
and connected via Firewire, iMovie will display the real-time image from
the camera. The import button will begin a capture that will save the video
footage directly to the hard drive of the computer. Clicking the import button a second time will stop the capture and make the clip available on the
shelf to the right of the monitor. This capture technique does not even require that the camera be loaded with tape. It is the quickest way to get
footage into the computer for editing and display. Using this setup, you can,
for the first time in classroom history, capture video footage in real time and
replay it without having to rewind tape. This instant access to video footage
is what makes the exercise in chapter 3 possible in the classroom.

Importing Nondigital Videotape into iMovie

Occasionally, you will want to import footage from a VHS or Hi8 tape to iMovie. To do this, you need an analogue-to-digital converter. Fortunately, your digital video camcorder can do this for you. There are also special pieces of equipment that can do this, and they are reviewed in chapter 8.

VHS and Hi 8 tapes save video using an analogue method, making an analogue-to-digital converter necessary. If your camcorder has pass-through capability you can plug the VCR or Hi 8 camera into your digital video camera's analogue port. Then plug your digital video camera into your computer using a Firewire cable (figure 6.5). Put the digital camera in VTR mode and press play on the VCR or Hi 8 camera. You will see the video appear on both the LCD screen of the camera and in the iMovie monitor. Click the import button to capture the footage directly to your hard drive. Click the import button a second time to stop the capture, and the clip will appear on the shelf ready for editing and integration into your digital video.

Figure 6.5   Connecting the Digital Video Camera to a VCR

To move a digital video from a DV camera and miniDV tape to a VHS tape, connect the camera to a VCR using RCA cables provided with the Camera. Set up the VCR to accept the composite signal from the camera, switch the camera to VTR mode, hit play on the camera, and record on the VCR.

Editing Video Footage

Naming the Clips

You may want to take the time to name each clip on the shelf at this point. They are by default named "Clip 1," "Clip 2," and so on. You can give them more descriptive names that will help you recognize and organize them. To do this, simply double click on the clip on the shelf and a clip info window will appear (figure 6.6). Change the name in the name field. You can also click once on the clip name on the shelf and change the name there.

Trimming Clips

Clips will need to be trimmed to eliminate the unwanted footage. It is important to note, however, that trimming in a digital, nonlinear editing system is "virtual" because the footage removed in the trimming procedure is not actually deleted. The program only changes the pointers in the video file to a new location on the footage and leaves the unwanted footage intact. This allows us to undo any overzealous trimming and restore the clip to its original state without having to recapture the footage.

To trim a clip, first select it on the shelf with a single click. This will bring the clip up in the monitor in edit mode. The scrubber bar appears

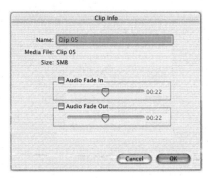

Figure 6.6   Clip Info Window

The Clip Info window allows you to re-name the clip and adjust the fade out du-ration times for the audio of the clip.

below the clip, and the playhead can be dragged along the scrubber in what is known as scrubbing through a clip. Notice that the numbers that appear next to the playhead are the minute frames of the clip. There are 30 frames in a minute in digital video, so you will see that the counter goes from 00:29 to 1:00. Using the left and right arrow keys, you can move a single frame at a time (1/30 second) through a clip for absolute precision in editing.

Once you have moved the playhead to exactly where you want to trim, hold the shift key and drag the playhead over the part of the video that you do not want. This will highlight the unwanted video in yellow. Diamond markers will appear at either end of the selected section. Move these markers by clicking and dragging them, or click on them and use the left and right arrows to move them one frame at a time (figure 6.7). To remove this section of video from the clip, simply hit the delete key on the keyboard or go to edit on the menu bar and select clear. This trims the clip of the unwanted footage.

If you regret having trimmed a clip and would like to restore the clip, choose the clip on the shelf and go to advanced on the menu bar, then to restore clip media. A dialogue box will ask you to confirm, then click restore.

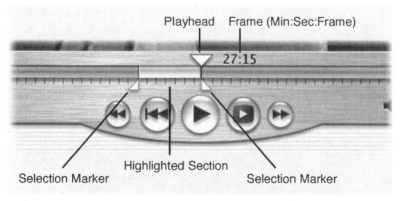

Figure 6.7   Highlighted Video Section on Scrubber Bar

You can highlight a section of video on the Scrubber Bar by holding the Shift Key and dragging the Playhead. Selection Markers appear and allow for further adjustments of the highlighted section. The numbers to the right of the Playhead indicate the frame you are looking at, displayed by Min:Sec:Frame. There are 30 frames per second (fps) in digital video.

Cropping Clip

Cropping clips is very similar to trimming. However, instead of selecting the area you do not want, you select the area you do want and disregard the rest. To do this, highlight the section of video you want from a clip by using the shift key and dragging the playhead to the end of the desired section of video. Then go to edit on the menu bar, then to cdit to crop. This will remove all but the highlighted section.

Duplicating a Clip

To duplicate a clip, simply click once on the clip on the shelf and go to edit and to copy. Then go to edit and to paste, and a clip with the same name will appear at the end of your clips on the shelf.

   To duplicate only a portion of a clip, highlight the segment you want to copy using the shift key and scrub the video, then go to edit and to copy, then edit and to paste. The clip will appear on the shelf in front of the original clip and be renamed (name of clip)/1.

Split a Clip in Two

There are times when you will want to split a clip into two clips. To do this, place the playhead at the point in the clip where you want the break and go to edit, then to split clip at playhead. This will split the clip into two clips on the shelf and create two different clips in the timeline.

Grabbing a Still Image from a Clip

You can save a frame from a clip as a still image in PICT or JPEG format in iMovie by moving the playhead to the frame you want to capture; going to file, then to save frame as; giving it a name; and choosing your format and location (figure 6.8). PICT image format is a lossless picture format, which means that all the information of a picture is saved for the best picture fidelity. The downside to PICT format is that the file size for each picture is large. JPEG is a lossee image format, which means that a compression algorithm is used to reduce the size of the picture; this causes some information and image fidelity to be compromised. Which format you choose to save the image in will depend on what you want to do with the

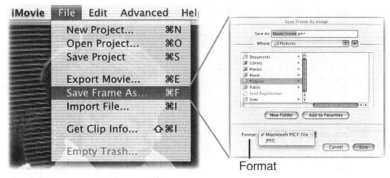

Format

Figure 6.8   Save Frame as Still Image

You can save a frame as a still image by using the File −> Save Frame As menu
option. In the Save dialogue box, choose an image format, Macintosh PICT File
or JPEG format. PICT is higher quality and larger in size. JPEG is lower in quality but more compatible with web and e-mail and is smaller in size.

image after it is saved. If you are going to post it to the web or e-mail it to
someone, file size is very important, so JPEG would be your better option.
If you are going to print the picture, import it back into iMovie, or edit it
further in an image manipulation program, file size is not as important but
image fidelity is important, making PICT the better file format.

Sequencing Clips from Shelf

You can sequence the clips on the timeline below in the clip view or timeline view by dragging the clips from the shelf to the timeline. Conversely,
you can remove clips from the timeline by dragging them out of the timeline in the icon view back to the shelf. You can change the order of the clips
by clicking, dragging, and dropping the clips in their new location on the
timeline. If you click on a clip in the clip view, the monitor will display the
clip and allow further trimming and cropping. To play the entire sequence
of clips as a video, either on the shelf or the timeline, click on the monitor
window and the monitor will display the video as a sequence of clips.

Adding Transitions

You can add transitions between the clips by clicking on the transitions
button at the bottom of the shelf, which brings up the transitions panel
(figure 6.9). Choose the type of transition and speed and use the preview

button to screen the transition. Once you have the preferred transition and speed, click and drag the transition between the relevant clips on the timeline. When the transition is in place, a little red line will appear below the clip indicating that the clip is being rendered. Rendering is the process by which the computer builds a clip frame by frame based on manipulations by the user. You need not wait for the rendering process to be completed before continuing, as iMovie will render in the background and allow many renderings to take place simultaneously.

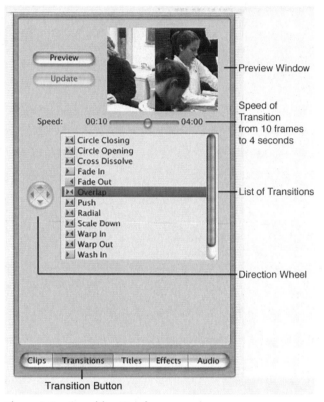

Figure 6.9   Transition Panel

The Transition Panel allows you to add transitions between clips in the timeline. Choose a transition from the list and adjust the duration using the Speed slider. Some transitions use the Direction Wheel to dictate the entry and path of the transition. Some transitions will have other options which will appear below the list. The Preview button will allow you to see the transition in the Preview window before you drag it to the timeline and render it.

Adding Titles

The title button on the shelf will bring up the title panel (figure 6.10), which will allow you to put words in your video either on top of video footage or over a black background. The words can appear in many different ways: flying, drifting, bouncing, or scrolling in from any side of the screen you choose, or simply appearing as a subtitle or centered text.

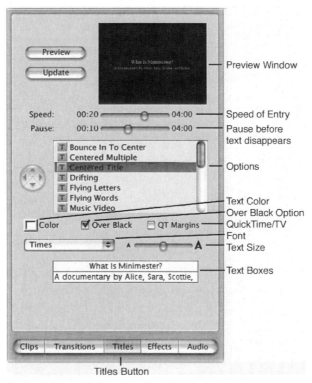

Figure 6.10   Title Panel

The Title Panel allows you to add text to your video. Choose your title option from the list and type the text into the text boxes below. Some options allow for more lines of text. You can change the speed, pause, text color, font, and text size in this window. If you choose the Over Black Option, once the option is dragged to the timeline, a new clip will be created for your title. If you do not check the Over Black Option, your text will be superimposed on the clip in which you drag the option. When QT Margins is left unchecked, the text will be moved away from the edges to avoid being cut off by TV overscanning.

Choose the type of title from the list, pick a direction you want the text to move using the direction wheel, select a font with the pulldown menu, and adjust the speed of entry and length of pause before the word begins to disappear using the speed and pause sliders. Also, adjust the size of the text using the font size slider, and color by clicking and choosing a color from the color box. Then type the text of the title in the boxes below. Some title options allow you to generate more lines of text than others.

By checking the over black box you will create a new clip with a black background. By leaving that box unchecked you will be able to superimpose the title on an existing clip.

The QT margins box allows you to control where on the screen the text will appear, to some degree. If your video is destined for viewing on a television screen, text needs to be moved in from the edges to make sure that it is not chopped off due to TV overscanning. If, however, your video is to be watched only as a QuickTime movie, you need not worry about overscanning, and checking this box will move the text closer to the edges.

Use the preview button to make sure the text appears as you like. When you are ready to apply the text to the video, drag a title option such as centered title from the list of options onto the timeline. If you are creating a title over black, drop the title option as you would any other video clip. If you are superimposing the text on an existing clip, drag the title option to the beginning of the clip. Doing this will apply the text to the clip from the beginning. If you would like the text to be applied to the middle of a clip, you must split the clip at the point at which you would like the text to begin. You may also have to split a clip if you would like to apply text to the beginning of a clip that already has a transition.

Once you click the apply button, a red line and numbers will appear below the clip as it renders the clip with the text. The numbers represent how many frames have been rendered and how many frames there are in all.

Adding Special Effects

The effects button brings up the special effects panel, which allows you to add special effects to your video footage (figure 6.11). You can apply special effects to a portion of a clip, an entire clip, or a portion of the video that spans multiple clips. First select the video on which you wish to apply an effect either by clicking on a clip, by making a selection on the scrubber bar using the shift key and dragging the playhead, or by holding the shift key down and selecting multiple clips by clicking on them.

Once you have a video selection, click on the effects button. There is a list of effects and corresponding options. The preview button allows you to view the effect before you click the apply button and begin a render. To undo an effect, simply use the restore button in the panel. You can apply more than one effect to a clip by choosing an effect, clicking the commit button, and then choosing another effect, and so on. Be careful when using

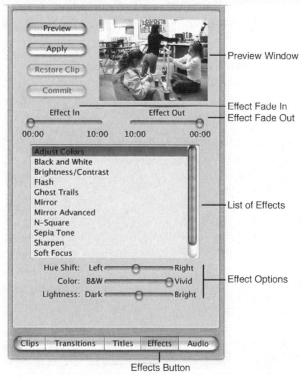

Figure 6.11   Effects Panel

The Effects Panel allows you to add special effects to your video. Choose from the list of effects and adjust the Effects Fade In and Fade Out time. Use the options under the list to create the effect desired. Preview the effect using the Preview Button at the top. To pile effect on top of effect, use the Commit Button to lock in place one effect before adding another. Click Apply when finished.

the commit button, because, once it is used, the restore clip button on the effects panel or restore clip media under the advanced menu option will no longer undo the applied effect. You can, however, import the clip again using the file and import file option: find the clip in the media folder of the project folder on the hard drive to bring in a new clip of the video in its original state.

Freeze Frame

To create the effect of freezing motion, use a combination of video footage and imported still images. First, move the playhead to the place on the video where you would like to freeze the motion. Second, split the clip at the playhead using the edit and split video clip at playhead options on the menu. Third, save the frame as a still image by using the file and save frame as menu options. Fourth, save the image as a PICT image to your hard drive and then import the still image back into iMovie using file and import file. This will import the still image as a five-second clip. Last, drag the clip off the clipboard into the timeline between the two clips you just split. This will make it appear as though the motion is frozen in place but, in reality, you will have created and inserted a clip of a still image.

Timeline View

The timeline view shows the video clips as well as the two additional audio tracks in proportional detail (figure 6.12). Using the zoom in/out pull-down option, you can zoom out to make the clips appear smaller, so that more of the clips are visible, or zoom in, so that the clips can be analyzed on a frame-by-frame basis. The 1x setting zooms out and lets you see the whole movie without having to scroll, while 50x zooms in and allows for a very close inspection of the clips.

In the timeline view you are able to adjust the volume of each clip by selecting it and using the volume slider. Unfortunately, you are not able to increase the volume of a clip in iMovie, only decrease it. On either side of the slider are checkboxes that allow you to fade in and out the audio of each clip. To adjust the length of the fade in and out, double click on the clip and use the fade in and out sliders in the clip info window (figure 6.6).

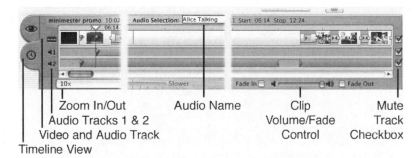

Zoom In/Out   Audio Name   Clip   Mute
Audio Tracks 1 & 2   Volume/Fade   Track
Video and Audio Track   Control   Checkbox
Timeline View

Figure 6.12   Timeline View

In the Timeline View you will see the Video Track and two Audio Tracks. The clips will be visible in proportion to their length. The Zoom pulldown allows you to zoom in and out for both bird's eye (1x), where you can see the entire video, and close inspection views (50x), where you can see each frame. The Volume slider allows you to adjust the volume of each video or audio clip.

The three checkboxes to the right of the three audio tracks are the mute buttons for each track, allowing you to turn off an entire audio track by unchecking the track you do not want to hear.

Fast, Slow, and Reverse Motion

The speed of a clip can be controlled in the timeline view by simply choosing and adjusting its speed using the speed slider adjustment. You will notice the clip will grow and shrink in the timeline view as you slide back and forth on the speed adjuster.

To make a clip play in reverse, select the clip and go to the advanced menu option and choose reverse clip direction.

Audio and Voice-overs

The audio button allows you to add sound effects, record your voice, or import music from a CD in the audio panel (figure 6.13). The panel is separated into three sections for sound effects, voice recording, and audio CD recording.

In the sound effects section, a list of provided effects is available to add to your movie by dragging those chosen down to one of the two audio channels.

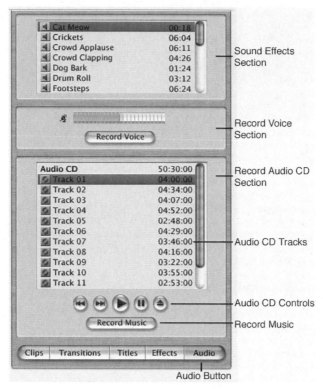

Figure 6.13   Audio Panel

The Audio Panel has three different areas, the Sound Effects Section, the Record Voice Section, and Record Audio CD Section. To add a sound effect, drag the desired effect from the list to one of the two audio tracks in the timeline. To record your voice, position the playhead on the video where you want to record and click the Record Voice button. To record music from a CD, insert the CD, choose the track, and click the Record Music button. To record only a portion of the song, use the play button and click the Record Music button to start and stop the capture at the beginning and end of the music segment.

   The record voice section allows you to record voice-overs. When recording your voice, you should watch the level on the computer meter and make sure you are speaking loud enough to make the level bump into the yellow and occasionally spike into the red. If your voice is not recording, or you would like to turn up the gain on the microphone so that you do not have to speak as loud, in OS 9.x go to the Apple menu, then to the sound control panel, then to the input tab. Make sure the correct microphone is selected and check the check signal level checkbox. You can then slide the gain slider while you talk to adjust the gain on the microphone. Set the gain so that the level bumps into the yellow and occasionally into the red while you are talking in a normal voice. Once this is set, return to iMovie and the microphone will be adjusted and ready for recording. Move the playhead to the area of the video you want to voice over and click the record voice button. The video will play in the monitor without sound, and a yellow bar will appear and grow in the first audio channel of the timeline view. This yellow bar represents your recorded voice. Talk through the voice-over and click the record voice button again to stop the recording.

To import music from a CD, insert the CD into the computer and the tracks will appear in the recording audio CD section. The play, pause, skip to next track, and eject buttons will control the CD. To record an entire track, select the track and click the record music button. This will start both playing the track and recording it. To capture only a portion of the track, use the play button to get to the section of the song you want, and then click the record music button to start the recording and click once again to stop the recording. While you are recording music, you will notice a purple bar growing in the second audio track of the timeline.

Adjustments to the volume of the voice-overs and imported music can be controlled in the same way the volume is controlled for the video clips. Click on the recorded audio clip in the timeline and use the volume slider to lower the volume to the desired level. Double clicking on the audio clip allows you to fade the recording in and out and adjust the speed of the fade.

The recorded audio can be moved around the video by dragging it along the audio tracks. It can be shortened by dragging the audio adjustment tabs at either end of the clip toward the center (figure 6.14). The clip can even be split by placing the playhead at the desired breaking point and using the edit and split video clip at playhead.

When you have the voice-over or music in the right place on the video, lock the audio into place relative to the video track. Move the playhead to the beginning of the audio clip, click once on the audio clip so that it

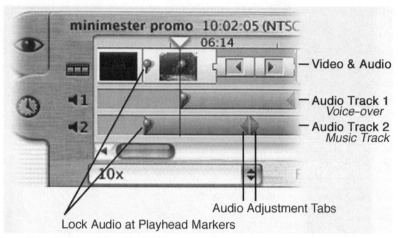

Figure 6.14   Timeline View

When the audio tracks are locked to the video track, markers in the shape of stickpins are visible in the audio and video tracks. Audio Adjustment tabs on both ends of each audio clip allow you to shorten the audible portion of the audio clip by clicking and dragging the tabs toward the center of the clip. Voice-over recordings are saved into Track 1 and music recordings into Track 2 by default. Audio that is not locked to video can be dragged around the video and even layered on top of each other in the same audio track.

is highlighted, go to the advanced menu option and then to lock audio clip at playhead. This will ensure that future video edits, which may move the video track around, will also move the recorded audio tracks. Locked audio tracks will be indicated by markers in the shape of stick pins tacked to the video and audio tracks (figure 6.14).

Another feature of the software is the ability to extract the audio from a video track. This is useful when you have recorded a sound effect on a digital video camera and want only the soundtrack of the video. Extracting the audio from the video also allows you to start with a clip of someone talking and then have another image appear while still hearing the person speaking from the first clip. To do this, highlight the video clip that has the audio you would like to extract and go to advanced, then to extract audio. This function will make a duplicate of the clip's audio, place it in a yellow bar in audio track 1, and turn the original clip's volume down to zero. You are then able to treat the extracted audio independently from the video track. You could even delete the video track, leaving just the audio of the clip in your video.

Export of Video from iMovie

iMovie allows you to export your movie to different formats for different distribution options. Under file and export, you have the option of exporting to camera, QuickTime, or iDVD (figure 6.15).

Export to Camera

When exporting video to a camera, you are saving a digital copy of the video that has no loss of quality. Once exported to the camera, the video can be copied from the miniDV tape to a VHS tape so that the movie can be watched on a VCR. Every camera has the ability to connect to a VCR using analogue RCA connectors. This allows you to have both a lossless copy archived on miniDV tape in digital format and a VHS copy that almost anyone can watch.

When exporting the video to the camera, iMovie "flattens" the movie. If you were to import the video back into iMovie from the camera, you

Figure 6.15   Export Movie

Export your video using one of the three options in the File to Export Movie option. Exporting the movie back to camera allows you to then copy the video to VHS tape and saves a lossless digital copy of your video for backup. QuickTime export allows you to turn your video into a computer file which can be shared with other computers via e-mail, web, or CD ROM. iDVD export prepares the video for import into iDVD where it can be burned onto a DVD disk.

would not be able to undo transitions, titles, or other edits. The video would come in as a video clip with all of the edits indelibly flattened into the clip.

Export to QuickTime

Exporting the movie to QuickTime format allows you to store your movie as a file that can be sent in an e-mail, streamed over the web, or stored on a CD ROM. You can even turn your movie into a video CD using an add-on program like Toast or Cleaner. The QuickTime Export gives you preset options in a pulldown list to accommodate the various forms of distribution. The expert option allows you to tweak the settings yourself (figure 6.16).

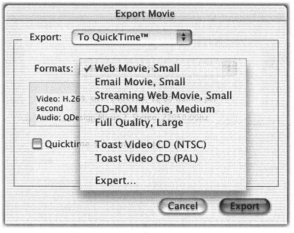

Figure 6.16   QuickTime Export

When choosing to export to QuickTime, you must also choose a distribution format from the Formats pull down menu. The options on the list are preset settings for each of the file distribution possibilities. All of the options, except Full Quality, Large, will reduce the file size of the video by reducing the playback window size, compress the video using a codec with various settings, and reduce audio quality. The Expert option allows you to manipulate each of these settings if you are so inclined. The Toast Video CD options are only available if you also purchase and install Roxio Toast 4 or better.

In the QuickTime Export option iMovie will compress the video, using a compressor called a codec and an audio compression format, so that it can be transmitted over the Internet or fit on a CD ROM. In reducing file size, the viewing size is reduced as well, to windows like 240 by 180 pixels, and the audio decreases from 48 kilohertz (KHz) to around 22 KHz (the more hertz the better in audio). Compression will also reduce the number of frames per second, from 30 to 10 or 12. With shrunken windows, decreased audio information, and fewer frames per second, there is a significant loss of quality. However, the loss of quality is necessary for distribution of video over the Internet or on CD ROMs, as discussed later in this chapter.

The preset options in QuickTime Export are optimal combinations for their stated purposes and should cover your different compression needs.

Export to iDVD

Exporting to iDVD is another preset of the QuickTime Export, using the DV-NTSC codec, but leaving the audio in uncompressed 48 Khz stereo. This setting makes sure the move is rendered and saves it as a stand-alone file that you drag and drop in iDVD to create a DVD disk.

IMOVIE EXTRAS

Companies have taken the opportunity to create additional filters, transitions, and special effects for iMovie. These additional programs add to the possibilities for your students' video creations. This flexibility becomes more important after your students have created their first few movies and find they are limited to the twelve effects provided by iMovie.

Virtix—Bravo, Echo, and Echo Effects

Virtix sells three products that add functionality to iMovie. Bravo is a special effects add-on program that gives you 20 special effects possibilities, from lasers and lightning strikes to fire and rain. Echo adds 18 transitions that allow a person to materialize or dematerialize in a flare of sparkle, or fog to roll in and out to reveal a new scene. Bravo and Echo are available as a package for $50.

For another $20, Zoom adds ten more special effects that allow you to do such things as zoom in and out of a video section or smudge a small portion of the video as if you were protecting the identity of a witness.

All three products are available for purchase at www.virtix.com.

GeeThree.com—Slick Transitions and Effects

For $50, you can add almost 100 new transitions and 20 new effects with GeeThree's Slick Transitions and Effects, volumes 1 and 2. Slick adds transitions such as page peel, whirlpool, and windshield wiper. Among the special effects are film noise, to make your video sound like a 50-year-old movie, and a camcorder effect, which puts the blinking "Rec" and brackets in the corners of the frame on the screen as though you were looking through the lens of the camcorder. These products are available for purchase at www.GeeThree.com.

eZedia—eZeMatte 1.0 for iMovie

eZeMatte from eZedia gives iMovie the ability to overlay images with holes in them on top of the video track and have the video visible through the holes. Ten of these masks are provided, and you are supplied with directions on how to create your own masks using Adobe Photoshop. This product is available at www.ezedia.com for $30.

PINNACLE STUDIO VERSION 7 OVERVIEW

Pinnacle Studio 7 is a highly functional digital video editor that will enable you to capture, edit, and export video into a variety of formats. As most PCs do not come with a Firewire connection, certain versions of Studio come with the Firewire hardware necessary to connect a digital video camera to your computer. Studio has more features than other consumer-level nonlinear digital video editors, which gives the program enhanced capabilities but also adds to its complexity. Mastery is still within the reach of high school students, although it takes a bit longer to teach them the program.

The manual that comes with Studio is very good and explains in detail all of the features of the program. I will, however, offer an overview here.

The program is set up with three different modes: capture, edit, and make movie, available via the tabs at the top of the main window. Each tab changes the configuration of the window and reveals different tools.

In capture mode, the program will import video from the camcorder and place clips in the album, while previewing the imported footage in the player window (figure 6.17). Each time you stop the import, the resulting clips are stored in a different folder, available via the dropdown menu or the folder icon in the album. The Diskometer allows you to change the set-

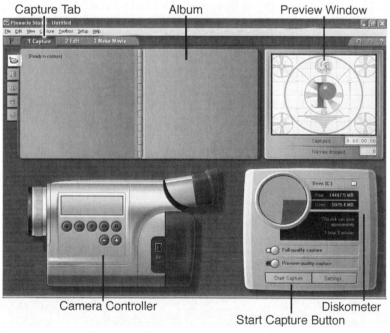

Figure 6.17   Studio-Capture Screen

Capture screen for Studio. The Camera Controller allows you to rewind, fast-forward, pause, and play the tape of the connected digital video camera using Firewire. The Start Capture button allows you to import video into the Album and preview it in the Preview Window. The Diskometer tells you how much disk space you have left.

tings of the capture from high quality to low quality and calculates how many more minutes of video your hard drive can handle.

The camcorder controller allows you to stop, rewind, play, fast-forward, and pause the camera using buttons on the digital video camcorder icon. The preview window allows you to view the contents of your tape as well as monitor the capturing of the video footage during import. When you want to capture the footage to the computer, use the start capture button in the Diskometer window to start recording. You will be prompted to name the group of clips you are about to import. When importing, the software will sense a break in the tape each time you stop and start the camera and will create an individual clip for each break. It is important that you read the directions in the manual to make sure there are no breaks in the time code caused by footage that is not contiguous—otherwise, importing the footage will be laborious and difficult. Use the same button, which during a capture will change to a stop capture button, to discontinue the capture.

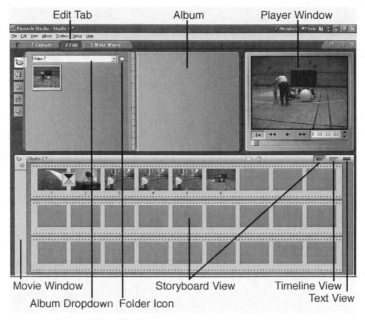

Figure 6.18   Studio-Edit Screen

In the Edit Screen, the Album holds the clips in groups under the drop-down menu or through the folder icon. The clips are dragged from the Album to the Movie Window which has three different views: Story-board, Timeline, and Text Views. The Player Window allows you to play a clip or the entire movie.

You have the option of capturing video at full quality or preview quality. Full quality will move the video from the camera to the computer with no loss of quality but will consume around 230 MB of hard disk space per minute. Preview quality is a low-resolution capture requiring much less disk space. However, when the project is completed and the video exported, the computer will recapture all of the required footage from the tape at full quality and apply all of the edits. Using the low-quality capture will add another step in the process, but it will save you hard disk space in the meantime, allowing for more projects to coexist on one computer.

In edit mode, you will have access to the captured footage on the album. Each group of clips will be available through the dropdown menu on the album (figure 6.18). Clips are dragged from the album to the movie window for sequencing. The movie window has three viewing options: storyboard, timeline, and text views. The storyboard view is helpful for sequencing the clips, but the most useful window is the timeline view (figure 6.19). In this view the video, audio, titles, voice-over, and music tracks are placed one on top of another. The first and second tracks are the video and audio track of the captured footage. The two can be manipulated together

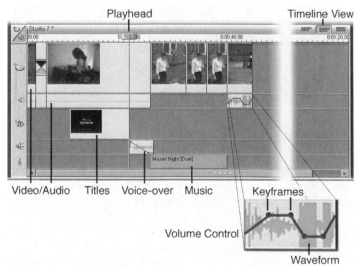

Figure 6.19 Studio-Timeline View

In the Timeline View, the Video, Audio, Titles, Voice-over, and Music tracks are stacked. The Audio and and Voiceover tracks draw a waveform so that you can see audio. Keyframes and a Volume Control line allow you to adjust the volume.

or edited individually. The third is the titles track, which allows words to be added to the video. The fourth track is for voice-overs, and the fifth track is for adding music from CDs or music files.

Two features of Studio that are usually reserved for higher-end video editors are the drawing of the waveform and the keyframe control in both the audio and voice-over tracks (figure 6.19). A waveform is the visual representation of the music. Being able to see the music's waveform means you can see the beat and match video clips to the music more easily and accurately. Keyframes in Studio are placeholders on a line that can control volume. By moving the keyframes up or down, you can raise or lower the volume of the track. In this way, you can adjust the volumes for various parts of different tracks at will.

Once you have edited the movie, you will use the make movie tab to access the export options (figure 6.20). Studio allows you to export the

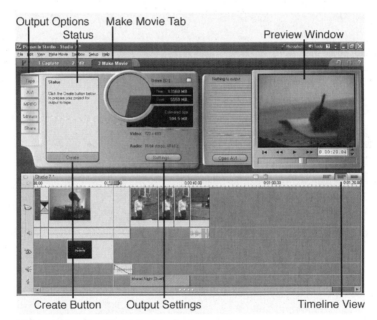

Figure 6.20   Studio-Make Movie Screen

In the Make Movie window, you have the option of exporting the movie to AVI format for other computers; MPEG to prepare the video for another application to make DVDs, VCDs, or CD ROMs; or Stream, which creates a video file in either RealAudio or Windows Media format for e-mailing or posting to the Internet.

movie to tape on the camera so that you can move it onto VHS tapes for VCRs or into an AVI file to be shared with other computers. It can also create MPEG 1 and 2 files, which can be burned as DVDs or VCDs using another piece of software like Ulead's DVD MovieFactory. The final options are to export the video to RealAudio or Windows Media files for streaming the movie over the Internet or e-mailing the files as a self-contained movie.

Pinnacle Studio version 7 is a strong program with some impressive features. It is not too difficult for students to use and will give them the tools for creating sophisticated videos.

PINNACLE STUDIO VERSION 8 OVERVIEW

Pinnacle Studio version 8 is a major update to version 7. The layout of the program is the same as that of version 7, with timelines and albums, but, under the hood, version 8 is very different.

Studio Version 8 is the first consumer-level nonlinear editing program I am aware of that can import and edit Sony's new digital video format, MicroMV. MicroMV is actually an MPEG2 format, the same format used in DVD disks. In programs like Studio version 7 and iMovie, the computer captures and manipulates video in a DV stream format, which takes up large amounts of disk space. It only compresses the DV stream video into MPEG2 just before it burns the DVD disk. In Studio Version 8, the program compresses the video into MPEG2 format as it is captured to the computer, or it accepts MPEG2 format natively from the camcorder.

Having the program capture and manipulate MPEG2 format video has advantages. First, it can now accept the MicroMV format. Second, less hard drive space is needed for each project because MPEG2 takes up about one-third the space that DV stream consumes. Third, the movie, once edited in MPEG2, is ready to be burned to a DVD directly.

Studio version 8 also has DVD-, VCD-, and SVCD-authoring capabilities built into it, eliminating the need for another program, such as Ulead DVD MovieFactory, to create a distribution copy of the video.

Studio DV version 8 is a worthy successor to version 7 and is an excellent program for student video productions.

Chapter Seven

Advanced Video Editing
and DVD Authoring Tools

ADVANCED NONLINEAR EDITING (NLE) PROGRAMS

iMovie and Pinnacle Studio version 7 and 8 are considered consumer-level digital video editors. They are appropriate entry-level video editing solutions for students. They are powerful enough to make professional-looking videos yet easy enough that teaching students how to use the programs takes little time.

However, there are many things that consumer-level programs cannot do. After your students have created a couple of movies, you and your students may be ready for more powerful tools that will allow you to take video editing to the next level. These advanced video tools, used by professionals and consumers alike, go by the name prosumer software. Prosumer nonlinear editing programs cost more money and have a much steeper learning curve.

Two such prosumer digital video editors are Apple's Final Cut Pro for Macintosh and Adobe's Premiere for Macintosh and Windows. These two programs offer greater control over the video and audio tracks and add functionality not available in iMovie or Studio. Final Cut Pro 3 for Macs, a $1,000 program favored by many professionals and broadcast stations, costs schools only $300 with an educational discount. Adobe Premiere for Macintosh and Windows is another favorite; it normally costs $550 but, with an educational discount, costs only $200.

The biggest difference between the consumer- and professional-level video editing programs is the ability to employ more than one video track. When you can layer video tracks on top of each other, many new possibilities open up. For one, it allows you to place a video inside another video. In this way you can have one video track of someone telling a story

Figure 7.1   Video-in-Video

**Multiple layers of video tracks available in prosumer
nonlinear digital video editing programs allow you to
show video-in-video pictures.**

while the rest of the screen can be devoted to some other footage, as is
demonstrated in figure 7.1. You can also layer multiple video tracks and
change the opacity of the layers so that more than one layer of video is
visible at the same time, as is demonstrated in figure 7.2.

Figure 7.2   Opacity

**Controlling the opacity of a video track allows you to
layer video tracks on top of each other and see through
the top video track into other video tracks below. In
this picture, the top video track is the Statue of Liberty,
layered on a video track featuring students.**

Having multiple layers of video also allows you to use Chromokey technology to replace the blue or green background of a video with a picture or another video. A video with a blue or green screen behind the subject is placed on the top video track. The program removes the blue or green background and creates a matte through which the video track below can be seen (figure 7.3). Chromokey is the technology used for meteorologists who, while standing in front of a blue screen on camera, appear to be standing in front of a weather map. Similar to Chromokey is the ability to use video clips that have an alpha channel—blank spaces in the video through which videos in subsequent layers can be seen. Digital Juice, discussed later in this chapter, is a company that

| Video Track 1 | Video Track 2 |

| Matte of Track 2 | Video Track 1 and 2 using Matte |

Figure 7.3   Chromokey

Chromokey technology allows you to layer two video tracks on top of each other and replace the background color of the top video track with the video track below. In this series of images, the underlying video track is a night shot of the Statue of Liberty. The top video track features a student playing a violin in front of a poster-board covered with blue paper. Using a special effect, you can create a matte on Track 2 by keying the blue of the screen and replacing it with the image below in Track 1.

provides hundreds of alpha channel videos and other innovative video resources.

Prosumer versions also enjoy advanced color and light correction tools that can improve the quality of poorly captured footage. In Final Cut Pro, there is an amazing three-point color correction process. You correct the color of a clip by clicking on a part of the picture that should be white, clicking on a part of the picture that should be black, and clicking on a part of the picture that should be grey; the picture corrects itself beautifully.

A standard feature of prosumer versions, which is also available in some consumer versions, is the drawing of the waveform of the audio track so that you can more easily match the clips to the soundtrack (figure 7.4). This is especially helpful when trying to match video to music. The beats are easy to find, as spikes on the waveform. When you scrub the movie by dragging the playhead across the scrubber bar, the audio track is audible, which helps you find precise locations in the video though the audio track—another useful feature.

Prosumer programs also give you greater control over different attributes of the video and audio tracks through the use of keyframes and value lines, which can adjust attributes over time—such as opacity, scale, and the position of the video on the canvas, to name but a few. In this way, you can fade music in slowly and have it fade out more quickly, as is shown in figure 7.4. Keyframes can also be used to change the size, rotation, and

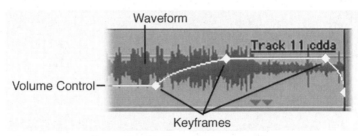

Figure 7.4   Audio Track with Waveform and Keyframes

With keyframes you are able to control the attributes of a video's audio track over time. In the figure above, keyframes have been added to the audio track to control the volume. The line connecting the keyframes is the volume value. The waveform of the audio is very helpful when working with audio.

position of a video clip along a defined path on the canvas of the screen. Almost every attribute that can be manipulated can be controlled through the use of keyframes.

In addition to the features that are not available in the consumer versions of video editing software, prosumer versions also have more of everything that the consumer versions do have, such as additional transitions, and special sound and video effects.

The potential exists for your students to learn professional-grade nonlinear editing programs. These programs will run comfortably on the same computers you would use for the consumer-level programs. It will, however, take commitment from you to master more complicated programs to be able to assist the students if they choose to learn these industry-strength programs.

If you do venture into these programs, you will probably only use them when students want to do something that is not possible with their entry-level editor. I show them how to use Chromokey technology, for example, with a prosumer-level editor and then export the rendered clip back to their entry-level editor, with which they are more familiar. What usually happens, however, is once they have used the prosumer version, they find it hard to go back to a program with fewer options, and choose to complete the video and produce future projects in the more advanced program.

Having a prosumer nonlinear editor in your pocket can open interesting options in a video project, but it is certainly not a necessary purchase. A more sophisticated program could even become an impediment if too much emphasis is placed on special effects instead of content or story. We see this all the time in movies that rely too heavily on special effects and give too little attention to plot or story development.

ADVANCED VIDEO AUTHORING AND COMPRESSION TOOLS

In addition to advanced video editors, there are many advanced video authoring tools that can add a truly professional look to any video. Using these programs, you can achieve broadcast quality effects, titles, backgrounds, and more.

Advanced Video Authoring Tools

Adobe After Effects—$300 with
Educational Discount

After Effects is an excellent tool to create animated graphics such as titles. Using After Effects, you can do such things as make three-dimensional letters tumble onto the video to create a title on the lower third of the screen. After Effects also works with layers of video so that you can layer video tracks on top of each other and change the opacity, allowing videos to be viewed through other video.

At the high end of what After Effects functions, you can build three-dimensional sets inside the computer and animate characters within the set using paths and keyframes. Your students can create an entire world within this program and have characters and objects move about it. They will be able to command perfect control of everything from source and intensity of lighting to camera placement and movement.

After Effects is an amazing program that will empower your students to create and control their own worlds within a video. The learning curve, however, is very steep, and only your most devoted and gifted video students will have the patience and ability to learn and manipulate this program. For more information visit www.adobe.com.

Digital Juice Jump Backs—$250
per Volume

Jump Backs are animated background videos that loop seamlessly behind CNN or Sports Center windows (figure 7.5). These backgrounds are three-dimensional backgrounds that have such things as turning globes and waving flags. Your students will love working with these tools to create the professional look they are used to seeing on TV.

Digital Juice Editor's Toolkit—$600

The Editor's Toolkit allows you to create animated lower third overlays, see-through animated overlays, as well as jump-back backgrounds (see above). Lower third overlays are the bars that appear beneath a talking head that identify the person (figure 7.6). These can be stationary or have

Figure 7.5   Animated Jump Back Backgrounds

Jump Backs provide professional looking backgrounds for picture in picture video.

a slight animation to them to catch the viewer's attention. Animated overlays are frames that go all the way around the subject (figure 7.7).

To create these backgrounds and mattes you have to use the Digital Juices software called The Juicer. This allows you to render all the clips to the specifications required and then layer them with other video tracks in an editor capable of multiple video tracks. You can find this and other useful video products at www.digitaljuice.com.

Compression Software

Compression software allows you to reduce the size of digital video so that it can be displayed on the Internet or moved to CD ROMs, VCDs, or DVDs. Many of the video editors will be able to export video into compressed formats, but compression programs give you greater control over the way in which the movie is compressed, and they employ more

Figure 7.6　Lower Third Overlays

Lower Third Overlays provide a professional way to add captions below the video.

Figure 7.7 Animated Overlays

Animated Overlays give you room to write on the screen and provide an interesting background. The center part is transparent allowing the underlying video to be visible through the overlay.

sophisticated algorithms to achieve superior results. These products really do help make your movie look good for lower-resolution formats like the web and CD ROMs.

Apple QuickTime 6 Pro—$30

QuickTime is the popular video format developed by Apple for distributing video over the Internet. QuickTime Player is available as a free download from the Apple website—for both Mac and Windows—and allows you to access many different video and audio formats. The Pro version of QuickTime, however, is a program that allows you to open almost any video or audio format and export that video or audio into almost two dozen different formats. It is therefore most useful as an inexpensive video- and audio-file converter. The most exciting of the formats QuickTime 6 can read and write is MPEG 4. MPEG 4 is a new format that allows you to compress very clean-looking full-screen video using just over 5 MB per minute, in contrast to the 230 MB per minute used by the camcorders and editors. QuickTime 6 Pro can be purchased online at www.apple.com/quicktime and comes free with Mac OS 10.2.

Sorenson Squeeze for QT—$275

Sorenson is a very popular compression engine used in other video editors. Sorenson also markets its own product, Squeeze, which does an excellent job of reducing the size of your video so that it can be viewed over the slow connections of the web. This program could hardly be easier to use. All you have to do is import the video into the program and tell it how you would like to use the compressed video file. Your options are choices like: over the Internet, with a modem, ISDN, broadband. The program then reduces the size of the movie accordingly. The preset options are optimized for their various delivery methods, or you can tweak the settings by hand for better results, if you know what you are doing.

Squeeze is only necessary if you will be displaying lots of your students' videos over the Internet. In that case, Squeeze will give you superior results with smaller file sizes than what your video editor is going to be able to accomplish.

Discrete Cleaner—$300 with
Educational Discount

Cleaner is another program used to convert and compress video into files that can be used for the web, CD ROMs, VCDs, and DVDs. This program is like Squeeze in that it allows you to compress the movie for any one of these specific purposes. Cleaner does a particularly good job of creating VCDs.

When compressing video with Cleaner, you can go with the defaults or tweak the settings yourself. Compressing video is still an art for those who do it professionally. Professionals use Cleaner to create the movie trailers and movie clips you see on the web, because it allows them to control all the settings for the compression, and the algorithms used are some of the best available.

Like Squeeze, Cleaner is only necessary if you plan to broadcast your students' videos over the Internet or through VCDs. In these cases, Cleaner will produce higher-quality Internet files and VCDs.

DVD AUTHORING SOFTWARE

DVD authoring software is necessary to move the video from the format of the video editor (DV Stream) to the format used by DVD disks (MPEG 2). This involves compressing the video from DV Stream, which takes up around 230 MB per second, to MPEG 2, which can hold about 90 minutes of high-quality video on a 4.7 GB disk. For the best compression into MPEG 2, I would direct you to the compression tool of Squeeze and Cleaner, listed above, but most DVD authoring tools do a more than satisfactory job.

DVD authoring tools are also necessary to build the navigation system for your DVD disk. The most basic authoring tool will just allow you to play the movies contained within, while more sophisticated authoring tools will allow you to jump into chapters and associate nonvideo content on your DVD disks like documents or programs.

The DVD authoring software also allows you to burn the digital content onto a DVD disk. For this, your software must be compatible with your DVD burner.

Apple iDVD—Free with Macintosh Computers with SuperDrives (Macintosh Only)

iDVD is a basic DVD authoring tool that comes free with Macintosh computers equipped with SuperDrives. iDVD works hand in hand with iMovie so that movies are exported out of iMovie into iDVD format, and then iDVD allows you to create the DVD disk. You can choose from a list of preconfigured backgrounds, fonts, and music for your menu page, or you can customize each to your preference.

iDVD also allows you to create up to six folders per screen so that you can create a navigation system (figure 7.8). Each folder can contain videos, still images, or more folders. You can associate an audio file with each folder so that when you go into each folder it has its own sound file.

Figure 7.8   iDVD example menu for DVD Disk.

iDVD lets you create a menu system for a DVD. This example has three folders, G1, G2, and G3 that have 2 videos each in them; a Scavenger Hunt video; and a Picture Album which has many still images that automatically advance to the music associated with the album.

A folder containing still images can be set so that the pictures rotate automatically or you have to step through each image using the DVD remote.

iDVD does not recognize burners other than the SuperDrive and does not allow you jump into a movie through chapter selections.

Ulead DVD MovieFactory—$50
(Windows Only)

DVD MovieFactory allows you to capture video from a DV tape, author menus, burn disks, and even make CD labels and covers. DVD MovieFactory is an excellent and necessary addition to Pinnacle's Studio 7 or any other Windows video editing solution that does not have DVD authoring and burning capabilities. Pinnacle Studio 8, however, has DVD authoring built into it, and therefore does not require DVD MovieFactory.

DVD MovieFactory can read your movie from a miniDV tape and detect scene changes and automatically create chapter thumbnails for future scene selection navigation. When creating the menu system, there are 38 templates to choose from, or you can customize your own. When you are ready to create a DVD disk, you can create an image from which you can burn many disks or go straight to disk by clicking "Create DVD."

DVD MovieFactory is an easy-to-use and intuitive program that picks up where the other video editors leave off. Thankfully, it is priced very reasonably and offers extra features like chapter selection and support for most up-to-date DVD burners.

Apple DVD Studio Pro—$500 with
Educational Discount (Macintosh Only)

DVD Studio Pro is Apple's professional-grade DVD authoring tool that allows you to create very sophisticated DVDs like the ones you rent or buy. A DVD disk has the ability to hold up to 16 language tracks, 32 subtitle tracks, 9 different camera perspectives, up to 36 buttons per menu with roll-over functionality (the buttons light up when selected), and built-in programs that can be played like games. DVD Studio Pro allows you to exploit all of the functionality available in a DVD disk and has the ability to write to many different DVD burners.

DVD Studio Pro is a much more complex program than its consumer cousins, iDVD and DVD MovieFactory. Unlike the consumer DVD authoring tools, DVD Studio Pro starts building a DVD from scratch, requiring you to specify every menu and create every link between buttons and other menus or videos. This degree of control offers greater flexibility but also adds significantly to the complexity of the process.

The beginner video enthusiast would do well to begin with the consumer DVD authoring tools and only graduate to the professional tools when he or she is totally frustrated by the lack of flexibility afforded by the consumer versions.

OTHER USEFUL UTILITIES

Your students' video-making experience will be more successful if you also have a few utility software packages. Here are two that are useful for working with video.

Roxio Toast and Easy CD Creator—$80 (Macintosh and Windows)

This utility comes in both Mac (Toast) and Windows (Easy CD Creator), and is useful for duplicating mastered DVDs. Just put a DVD you created into the computer and Roxio's programs will create disk images that you can then use to create identical duplicates.

This utility also has a label-maker program that helps you create CD jewel case covers and inserts and CD labels. These final touches are a great improvement over handwritten labels and cases.

Norton Utilities—$50 to $100 (Macintosh and Windows)

It is imperative that you keep your hard disks healthy when working with video as explained in Chapter 6. No application taxes your hard drives like video. Fragmented disks and slow disk access speed account for a vast majority of crashes when working with video. Therefore, it is very important that you run disk utilities and defragging programs on your computer hard drives often. Disk utilities will look for bad sectors of the hard drive. If any are found, begin to think about replacing the drive soon. Bad sectors are an indicator that the disk is about to fail.

Defragging a disk cleans up the disk and makes it easier for the computer to write information to the disk quickly and find the information it needs. As you use the computer and delete and save new files, the computer frees up space on the disk where the deleted file used to be. Then the computer reuses those free spaces on the disk for its next file save. If you try to write a large file like video to a disk that has lots of little spaces on the disk where little files used to be, the computer is forced to jump around the disk and write a little information here and a little information there, sometimes causing the computer to freeze while importing. Defragging a disk will reassociate the fragments of files that are already on your computer and pack them together at the beginning of the disk, creating large open spaces at the end of the disk. Once defragged, your computer will be able to write large video files to the hard drive more quickly because it will not have to jump around looking for another free block, minimizing the potential for disk related crashes. The process of defragging a disk takes a lot of time so I suggest launching the process before you leave at night and having it defrag after hours.

Chapter Eight

Distribution Formats

Your choices for distributing your videos are these: DVD, VHS, video CD (VCD), miniDV tape, CD ROM, or the web. Each format has its advantages and disadvantages. The follow section reviews each format and rates them on a five-point scale for expense, compatibility with equipment, video quality, and duplication speed. The expense category rates how costly it is to duplicate a video for your audience. The cost per copy ranges from almost free to $5 per copy. Compatibility with home equipment evaluates how likely it is that the members of your audience will be able to view your video on the given distribution format. Video quality rates the aesthetic and auditory fidelity of the video once moved to the distribution format. Video quality is often measured in horizontal lines, the highest quality of video for our purposes being the 720 lines enjoyed by DV tape, compared to VHS, which has only 240. The last category of measure is duplication speed, which rates the format on how quickly duplicates can be made. With VHS, unless you have a high-speed duplicator, only one copy can be produced in the time it takes to watch the video, known as real time. While CD ROM reproduction takes more time to create the first disk, subsequent disks can be made in a fraction of the time it would take to watch it in real time.

Scale: Very Poor ○○○○○ Excellent ●●●●●

VHS

Expense	●●●○○
Compatibility with Home	●●●●●

Video Quality   ●●●●○
Duplication Speed   ●●○○○

VHS remains the best distribution format available for now. It is relatively inexpensive, at around $2 per copy, and has the highest compatibil-
ity with the students' home systems; almost everyone has a VCR to view
VHS tapes.

VHS has its limitations and drawbacks. When video is transferred from
the computer to VHS, there is some loss of video quality, from 720 lines
of information on DV down to 240 lines for standard VHS. However,
since we are all used to and accept the resolution of VHS tapes, this is not
much of a limitation. A drawback is that it can only be played linearly
from beginning to end, which makes the medium less conducive to putting multiple presentations on one tape. Potentially, viewers would have
to fast-forward through a number of presentations to the one of interest on
the tape. Duplication of videos from the computer happens in real time,
and the process has to be monitored, making sure that tape is rewound, the
VCR is set in record mode and on the right channel, and so on. VHS tapes
are also bulky and awkward. These aspects are not necessarily seen as
limitations until the medium is compared to another like DVD.

DVD

Expense   ●●○○○
Compatibility with Home   ●●○○○
Video Quality   ●●●●●
Duplication Speed   ●●○○○

DVD will undoubtedly become the standard distribution format in the
near future. Its current drawbacks are that many people do not have DVD
players yet and that the blank DVD disks are still expensive, at approximately $5 per disk. However, DVD player sales have skyrocketed re-
cently and prices of players and blank DVD media are falling. We will see
a repeat of the declining cost of the blank CD ROM disk, which only a
few years ago cost $6 per disk and now costs next to nothing.

DVDs enjoy a much higher video resolution and sound fidelity, on top of supporting a menu-driven navigation system that allows instant access to all parts of the disk. Menu navigation enables you to place many videos on one disk, unlike burying one video behind another on a tape. A menu is especially useful for classes in which you would like to include everyone's projects but want to make sure each group can easily access their own project.

You also have the option of placing still images on a DVD so that students can have a photo album as well as video. You can include a folder full of digital images taken from a digital camera. Using the remote control of a DVD player, you can scroll through images individually, or, with some programs, you can create a slide show in which the images automatically advance. You can even add a soundtrack to your slide show.

To burn a DVD disk, your computer must encode the video and stills in MPEG 2 format, which is a compression scheme. The time it will take your computer to compress the video into MPEG 2 will depend on the speed of your computer and program. Once the compression of the video is complete, each disk will take about 30 percent longer than the presentation length of the video to burn.

Within a few years VCRs and VHS tapes will go the way of the vinyl record album and 8-track tape. In addition to better picture and sound quality, superior navigation, and inclusion of still images, DVDs enjoy a smaller and more manageable form factor than their VHS brothers. I look forward to the day when DVD is the standard, the disks are less expensive, and the burners duplicate in a fraction of their current time.

VIDEO CD (VCD)

Expense	●●●●●
Compatibility with Home	●●○○○
Video Quality	●●●○○
Duplication Speed	●●●●●

VCDs are inexpensive cousins of DVDs. They are movies encoded in MPEG 1, which has a lower resolution than MPEG 2 and a correspondingly smaller file size. This smaller file size allows movies to be put on inexpensive blank CDs. This format has not been as popular in America as it has been in Asia. The beauty of this format is the inexpensive nature of the media required, and the use of regular blank CDs, which are averaging $0.20 per disk and, in some cases, are almost free with rebate.

There are two options for viewing VCDs: certain DVD players and computers. Computers can play VCDs using VCD software. A search on www.shareware.com for VCD will result in a dozen or more programs for all platforms; they can be purchased online for as little as $10 and downloaded. Some versions of QuickTime and Windows Media Player will also allow you to watch some VCDs. All but the very low-end new DVD players have the dual-wavelength laser necessary to play the VCDs you create on your computer.

VCDs lack a menu navigation system like that on DVDs, acting more like VHS tapes in that they can only be played linearly. Once a disk is inserted, your options are limited to play, fast-forward, and rewind. If multiple videos were placed on a VCD, the user would be required to fast-forward to reach the desired videos.

To create a VCD you may need an additional software package like Roxio's Toast, version 4 or greater, for Mac, or Roxio's Easy CD Creator for Windows. I have found the video quality of VCDs in some cases to be less than desirable. The limited availability of DVD players that can handle VCD, as well as the additional requirement of special software for viewing VCDs on computers, make VCD a less attractive option. Its only advantage over DVD are the inexpensive disk and the speed at which VCDs can be duplicated. Because you are burning a regular computer disk, your 40x burner will be able to turn out VCDs at a surprisingly fast rate. However, as the price of blank DVDs goes down and the speed of DVD burners increases, the viability of VCDs will decline. For now, VCDs remain a quick and inexpensive solution for those users who are tech savvy enough to load the proper software on their computers or are fortunate enough to have the latest DVD players.

CD ROM

Expense   ●●●●●
Compatibility with Home   ●●●○○

Video Quality	●●○○○
Duplication Speed	●●●●●

Exporting your video to a proprietary format like QuickTime, Real Audio, or Windows Media Player allows you to distribute video on CD ROMs. Almost all computers have programs that can play these formats. The players for these formats can even be distributed for no cost on the same CD as the video to ensure the viewer's ability to play the contents of the CD.

However, these formats require a great deal of compression, which degrades the video quality. If the video is longer than a few minutes, significant compression will be necessary, which will, in turn, reduce the size of the window in which the video can be viewed. This seriously degrades the quality of video and sound reproduction.

The true strength of these formats is not in their fidelity but in their ability to combine varied materials on the same CD. In this way, a CD can be used to portfolio a student's papers, PowerPoint presentations, images of artwork, and small videos. Because these formats are burned on a regular CD, they can be quickly mastered on an inexpensive disk.

INTERNET/WEB

Expense	●●●●●
Compatibility with Home	●●●○○
Video Quality	●○○○○
Duplication Speed	N/A

Distributing videos on the web is an almost free way to reach a huge audience. Once a video is posted to the web, virtually any person in the world connected to the Internet can view it. A computer must have the appropriate software to view the downloaded movie, but most computers connected to the web today come preloaded with these programs, or the programs are free to download.

However, the video will need to be significantly compressed to shrink the file size to accommodate the slow speed of most people's connection to the Internet. This extreme compression considerably degrades the quality of the video, reducing the image to the size of a postage stamp on the screen. Even with a compressed file, students at home with slow modems will have to wait a long time for the movie to download to their computers. Cable Internet and DSL connections help a great deal, and more and more families are availing themselves of these services, but these households are still a small minority. Care must be taken to make sure that the web server hosting the video enjoys a fast connection to the Internet, or you risk delaying the download speeds even more.

All of these drawbacks do not change the fact that, until recently, students were not able to distribute their video material in such a democratic fashion. It is truly a publishing revolution when your students can make a video and instantaneously share it with the world.

MINIDV TAPE

Expense	●○○○○
Compatibility with Home	●○○○○
Video Quality	●●●●●
Duplication Speed	●●○○○

MiniDV is not so much a distribution format as it is an archival method. MiniDV decks or players are very rare, given that they cost more than most miniDV cameras and that the camera can double as a deck. When given the choice of a miniDV deck, which is permanently connected to the computer, or another miniDV camera, which can be both a camera and a deck, most people opt for the additional camera. While it is inconvenient to unplug the camera from the computer for playback and export, you will have another camera to lend to students and teachers. It only makes sense to get a dedicated deck when you are using expensive cameras and you want to protect the heads of the cameras by saving them the work of acting like a tape player.

MiniDV is the best way to archive your finished product because the video does not go through any type of compression when transferred back and forth between the camera and computer. It therefore is a lossless (no loss of information) copy of the original. If you edit in the future, you have the option of transferring the edited video back to the computer and continuing work on it. You cannot, however, undo the effects, transitions, or titles applied to the original.

When I move final products back to tape, I put them on a separate tape from the one used to capture the raw footage and designate them "Final Cuts Tape X." Then I either archive the raw footage tape, if I think there will be a need for further editing, or tape over it with other projects. Tapes need to be retired after multiple uses when aberrations appear on the tape—small squares that occasionally pop up and are caused by bits of data not being properly stored.

CONCLUSION

You have many choices when deciding how to distribute your students' video projects. An inexpensive and widely accessible video medium is the VHS tape. VHS tape offers a good quality picture that everyone can take home and play. DVD will be the distribution format of choice soon. It has higher resolution, better sound quality, and a menu-driven interface for quick access to multiple presentations contained on a single small disk. A few more Christmases like the last, in which DVDs were big sellers, and you will be able comfortably to switch to DVD. In the meantime, I take orders from students who want VHS tapes as well as those who want DVD disks.

VCDs are becoming a viable, inexpensive option as more students get DVD players, but the benefit of the less-expensive medium has to be weighed against a lower-quality picture and lack of menu navigation. As blank DVD disks drop in price, the balance will tip in DVDs' favor. Distributing video in QuickTime, Real Audio, and Windows Media Player formats on CD ROM is another option, especially if you want to combine it with other computer files. At the risk of confusing you, I will mention that you can also distribute these formats on a data DVD disk, which can store 4.7 GB of information, as opposed to the 700 MB you are limited to on a blank CD ROM disk. The extra storage capacity of the data DVD is very useful for archiving a student's works in a portfolio, which could easily consist of multiple QuickTime videos, PowerPoint presentations, pictures of art projects, digital art, and papers.

Video on the web offers the exciting possibility of reaching a large audience. Image and sound quality are greatly compromised, but the potential audience may be worth the price. I frequently use the web for distribution in combination with other methods.

I always make sure to archive video projects to miniDV tape. This lossless storage method allows for future copies to be made or edits to be done at the resolution of the original footage.

Chapter Nine

Camcorders

The camcorders available today come in many different formats and with a dizzying array of options. I will be focusing on the digital video formats, given that they work best with the nonlinear editing software discussed earlier. Digital video also enjoys a higher resolution image that does not degrade as it is transferred from generation to generation of duplicates. Digital video uses tapes that save the video images in series of ones and zeros that can be passed from camcorder to computer and back again with no loss of information or quality.

Most of the camcorders today also have the ability to capture still images, but the camcorders are still not as good as the regular digital cameras, which take higher-quality still images and do not cost as much as the camcorders. It is convenient, however, to have still capture capabilities built into the digital video camcorder. The still images can be saved to the digital videotape or onto a removable memory card. These memory cards come in three flavors for varying amounts of memory. Your camcorder manufacturer will dictate which type of card you will use, but they all work the same way.

The following section will review the different formats and features available on camcorders today and discuss the features that are most important to educational video. Three specific camcorders that are particularly well suited for educational video are reviewed below. I would not suggest getting a camcorder that costs less than the following models, as it will lack features you will discover important. If you have the resources, you could certainly purchase models superior to the ones reviewed and enjoy better picture quality and additional features.

You can still use the VHS, 8mm, and Hi8 analogue camcorders to capture footage, but you will then also need a digital video converter to transfer the video from its analogue source into a digital format for the computer. Two of these units are reviewed, and what they do explained at the end of the chapter. Below are the different aspects of a camcorder you will want to take into consideration when choosing the unit that will best meet your needs.

DIGITAL VIDEO FORMATS—MINIDV OR DIGITAL8

Presently, the two digital video formats of interest to educational video are miniDV and Digital8. MiniDV is the more prevalent of the two formats, but Digital8 is a less expensive consumer video format.

MiniDV is an excellent choice for educational purposes. It is a recognized standard and many manufacturers make models ranging from $400 to $5,000 and up. MiniDV is inexpensive enough to be affordable for educational and amateur use, yet robust enough to be useful to professionals.

Digital8 is a consumer-level format that allows you to save digital video on inexpensive Hi8 tapes. Digital8 camcorders are also backwardly compatible with analogue Hi8 and 8 mm tapes, which is especially helpful if you have an existing library of such tapes. The Digital8 camcorders are less expensive, but are also larger and in most cases have lower resolutions than their miniDV counterparts. As miniDV camcorders continue to drop in price, they appear to be squeezing out the Digital8 format. Many manufacturers have dropped the Digital8 format and focused on the miniDV format instead.

Sony has announced a new format, MicroMV, that enjoys many new and useful features. This new format is three times more efficient, allowing you to save much more video per megabyte than miniDV. The tapes are tiny and equipped with a chip that indexes the clips on the tape with an icon of the first frame, allowing you to jump from take to take more easily. Because the tape is smaller, the camcorders can be made smaller, some of them so small they could easily fit in a breast pocket. Unfortunately, this format is not compatible with the digital video editing programs discussed in this book, except Pinnacle Studio version 8, and the camcorders and tapes are still too expensive for educational institutions to justify.

RESOLUTION AND COLOR REPRODUCTION

Digital camcorders use a chip called a charge coupled device (CCD) to capture the image behind the lens. A CCD has thousands or millions of pixels that translate the image it receives into a digital picture; the more pixels, the higher the resolution, the sharper the picture. A camera with 300,000 or more pixels is more than adequate to capture a sharp picture with decent color reproduction. If it is important to you for the camcorder to also be able to capture high-quality still images, you will want to look for a camcorder with lots of pixels, a megapixel (1 million pixels) or more.

More expensive camcorders, like the ones used by professionals, have three CCDs, each dedicated to capturing red, green, or blue light. These multichip camcorders enjoy greater accuracy and range of color representation. They are expensive for student use, starting at $1,600. All the camcorders reviewed in this chapter are single-chip units that do a more than adequate job of color and resolution reproduction.

FIREWIRE, iLINK, AND IEEE 1394 CONNECTIONS FOR TRANSFER OF VIDEO

The camcorder must have a way to transfer the digital video from the camcorder to the computer and back again. This is achieved through an IEEE 1394 connection. This connection goes by different names. Canon simply calls it IEEE 1394, Sony and Panasonic call it an iLink port, and most computer manufacturers call it Firewire. These products all refer to the same standard set by the IEEE organization. They are only named different things to avoid paying royalties to IEEE's creator, Apple.

MEMORY CARDS FOR STILL IMAGES

Every camcorder, except the very low end, is equipped with a memory card for saving the still photos taken in memory mode. These cards differ depending on the manufacturer. Sony has its own Memory Stick, while Canon and Panasonic use MultiMediaCards[t] and SD Memory Cards for storing digital still images. The larger the capacity of the card, the more images you will be able to store on the camcorder. Extra cards can be purchased for additional storage capacity.

Optional memory card readers, usually sold separately, connect to your computer and allow your computer to read the contents of the card as if it were a floppy disk.

USB CONNECTIONS FOR STILL IMAGES

A USB connection on the camcorder is the most convenient method of accessing the still images. Using this connection, you plug the camcorder into the computer using a USB cable, and the computer mounts the memory card on your computer and allows you to read and write to the card as if it were a floppy disk.

ZOOMS—OPTICAL AND DIGITAL

Digital camcorders offer two types of zooms, optical and digital. The optical zoom is governed by the physical limitations of the lens. When zooming in using the optical zoom, the lens is adjusted to enlarge the picture and the resolution remains constant throughout. The digital zoom, on the other hand, magnifies the picture beyond the physical limitations of the optical zoom, by magnifying the digital picture within the camera. As the camera employs the digital zoom, the picture will begin to break down into identifiable pixels that look like blocks of color, making a mosaic of pixels—the same way a picture becomes pixilated when you enlarge it on a computer screen.

PROGRESSIVE VS. INTERLACED SCAN

Interlaced video is the standard in video: each frame is comprised of a combination of two pictures, one picture composed of the odd lines and one of even lines. The camcorder first takes the odd lines of the picture and then the even lines. The two fields are combined to make up each frame. This works well for video. However, interlaced video presents a problem when you are trying to extract still images from the video. In these cases, the odd and even lines will not match up, especially if there is fast movement in the picture.

Progressive mode, on the other hand, takes each frame as an entire picture at one time. This is the native format for digital TV and is the future of video. Progressive is a superior format, especially for freeze-frame video, because each frame is its own picture, not the combination of two half pictures taken at different times. Progressive mode video is also more easily converted to other computer-based video formats such as Quick-Time, video CDs, and DVDs.

It is not imperative your camcorder have progressive scan capabilities, unless crisp freeze-frames are somehow critical to your students' video projects, but it is a nice feature to have.

SHOE ATTACHMENTS FOR ACCESSORIES

Some camcorders come with a plate with rails on the top, called a shoe, that allows you to attach a flash, light, or external microphone (figure 9.1). These shoes are convenient for the single camera operator, allowing the peripherals to be attached to the camera as opposed to having to be held separately. The

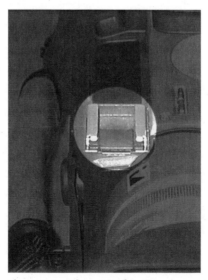

Figure 9.1   Shoe Attachment

more advanced shoe plates, called hot or intelligent shoes, have connectors that permit the camcorder to power, control, and accept input from the attached device, without wires or another source of power. The convenience does have a cost, however, as the hot shoe attachments draw power from the camcorder battery, shortening its life between recharges.

IMAGE STABILIZATION

The image stabilization feature on each camcorder attempts to smooth out the shake caused by hand movement. Almost every camera has this feature and each manufacturer goes about achieving this result differently. Be aware that, when on, this feature draws extra power from the battery. Consequently, it should be turned off if you are using a tripod and do not need the extra stabilization.

NIGHT VISION

Night vision is a feature offered on many camcorders that uses infrared beams to illuminate the picture in low light or complete darkness. The effect is similar to that of the night vision goggles used in the military.

Caution your students about harming the camcorder by dropping it or tripping while operating in total darkness. While this is a neat feature and creates an interesting effect, it is not altogether necessary.

ANALOGUE-TO-DIGITAL PASS-THROUGH

One way to convert analogue to digital video for editing on the computer is through a two-step process of connecting a VCR to a camcorder, using the camcorder's analogue inputs, and recording the VHS tape to digital tape. Then it's possible to import the digital video from the digital tape into the computer using the IEEE 1394 input.

A simpler one-step process is available with camcorders that have pass-through capabilities. The camcorder is connected to both the VCR, using the analogue inputs, and to the computer, using the Firewire port (figure 9.2). The camcorder then reads the analogue information, converts it to

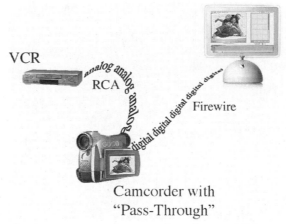

VCR

RCA

analog analog analog

digital digital digital digital digital

Firewire

Camcorder with
"Pass-Through"

Figure 9.2   Camcorder "Pass-Through" Capabilities

digital video, and passes it to the computer over its Firewire connection. In this way the analogue-to-digital converter translates video on the fly into a digital format for the computer without the need for a digital tape.

FORM FACTOR

The ergonomics of the camera should also be considered. For instance, the buttons and controls should be positioned in such a way that your students are able to operate the camcorder comfortably with one hand. This can only be tested in a showroom, where you will be able to pick up each camcorder and try it for yourself. If possible, have an average sized student go with you to see how his or her hands fit around the camera as well. Some cameras are definitely easier to hold and operate with one hand than others.

Another form factor consideration is size, with the premium placed on smaller units that weigh less and are easy to store. In the case of education, however, there is such a thing as too small. The smallest of the camcorders available are too costly and delicate for classroom use. When manufacturers have to pack everything into a case that fits into your breast pocket, the components are correspondingly smaller and more costly to produce and repair. Also, as camcorders get smaller, there is less space for buttons and controls on the exterior of the camera, forcing many useful functions into the menu system of the camera. Navigating a menu system on a camcorder for commonly used functions can be a hassle and add to the complexity for the user, requiring more training and a steeper learning curve.

Look for a camcorder that is small and light that will be easy for your students to use one-handed, but not so small that you worry about loosing it in your desk drawer.

CAMCORDER REVIEWS

Below are reviews of one Digital8 and three miniDV camcorders that are appropriate for education, having all of the desired features and street prices under $700. Each of these camcorders does a great job at capturing video footage under a variety of lighting conditions. I recommend these camcorders as the base models that schools should consider. More-expensive camcorders will certainly have more features, superior lenses, higher resolutions, and better color representations. Less-expensive camcorders will lack features you may find important.

Please also keep in mind that this is a mere sampling of the camcorders available, and the models will invariably change. Manufacturers come out with new models frequently, replacing their previous models with ones that have more capabilities and a lower cost. MiniDV camcorders have been coming down in price by about $100 per year while adding to the feature list and improving their performance.

The desired features common to each of the following cameras are:

- Image stabilization
- Excellent picture and recording capabilities
- Still photo capability with a memory card for storage of still images
- IEEE 1394 connection to transfer digital video between the camcorder and computer
- USB connection for accessing the still images on the memory cards
- External microphone in jack for connecting an external microphone

What separates the consumer camcorders from the prosumer- and professional-level camcorders is the number and quality of chips they use to capture the image. The consumer-level camcorders have only one chip, or CCD, while the next-level camcorders have three CCDs.

Following are reviews for four educationally appropriate, single-CCD camcorders and a comparison table (table 9.1). See table on page 164. In alphabetical order, the camcorders are:

Canon ZR50MC—MiniDV

Canon is a top manufacturer of digital camcorders for consumers and professionals. Their ZR series camcorders have enjoyed good reviews and solid performance since their introduction in 1998. The Canon ZR50MC is the latest iteration in that line and is well suited for classroom use (figure 9.3).

The ZR50MC is the top of the ZR line of camcorders, with the standout features of a whopping 22x optical/440x digital zoom and an advanced accessory shoe. The zoom on this camera gives it binocular-like capabilities that, when fully employed, require a tripod to keep the image stable. The advanced accessory shoe is a hot shoe that allows you to connect a microphone or video light without extra wires or batteries.

The optional shotgun microphone that goes in the hot shoe is a superior mike that can double as a unidirectional (shotgun) mike, which is only sensitive to sound directly in front of it, and an omnidirectional microphone, which picks up sound from all sides equally.

The ZR50MC is the smallest and lightest of the three camcorders and has the best ergonomic design, in my opinion. The camcorder fits more

Figure 9.3   Canon ZR50MC; Credit: Canon

comfortably in the user's hand and the buttons are more easily accessible, especially for students with smaller hands.

Panasonic PV-DV402—MiniDV

Panasonic is a huge manufacturer of camcorder equipment, with an impressive selection of miniDV camcorders—14 at last count. The PV-DV402 is about one-third the way up the Panasonic hierarchy and is advantaged by a large (3.5-inch) LCD screen, megapixel still images, a built-in light, and infrared night vision capabilities (figure 9.4).

This camcorder begins to bridge the gap between camcorders and digital still cameras. Its megapixel still capabilities allow it to take high-resolution pictures like the ones that you would expect from a low-end digital camera. This camcorder also has a built-in light, which would be standard on digital still cameras, but is lacking on the other digital camcorders in this category. The built-in light is especially useful, since it acts as an additional light for taking video or still images.

Sony DCR-TRV18—MiniDV

Sony has an outstanding reputation as a maker of electronic equipment, so much so that some people would not think of buying anything but Sony. This model comes with the Carl Zeiss lens, intelligent accessory shoe, and Nightshot capabilities (figure 9.5). It is the entry-level camera in the Sony line of miniDV camcorders. The features and capabilities expand as you ascend Sony's impressive lineup of miniDV camcorders.

I did find the TRV18 to be one of the more difficult cameras to operate with only one hand. The record button was too high up the back

Figure 9.4   Panasonic PV-DV402; Credit: Panasonic

Figure 9.5   Sony DCR-TRV18; Credit: Courtesy of Sony Electronics, Inc.

to comfortably reach with my thumb while I supported the camcorder from below.

Sony makes flashes and lights for the intelligent accessory shoe. They even make an infrared light that can extend the Nightshot range from 10 feet to 100 feet.

Sony DCR-TRV740—Digital8

This Digital8 format offers an impressive list of features for the cost. The DCR-TRV740 is one step away from the top model in the Digital8 line of camcorders from Sony (figure 9.6). It is backwardly compatible with 8mm

Figure 9.6   Sony DCR-TRV740; Credit: Courtesy of Sony Electronics, Inc.

Table 9.1   Comparison Chart for Camcorders

	Canon ZR50MC	Panasonic PV-DV402	Sony DCR-TRV18	Sony DCR-TRV740
Format	miniDV	miniDV	miniDV	Digital8
Lines of Resolution	500	500	500	520
Optical Zoom	22x	10x	10x	15x
Digital Zoom	440x	700x	120x	420x
Video Pixels	480,000	680,000	340,000	690,000
LCD Screen	2.5″ Color	3.5″ Color	2.5″ Color	2.5″ Color
Viewfinder	Color	Color	Color	Color
Digital Still Resolution	640x480	1280x960	640x480	1152x864
Media Card	8MB MMC	8MB SD	8MB MS**	8MB MS**
Progressive Mode	Yes	No****	Yes	Yes
Night Vision w/Infrared	No	MagicVu™	Nightshot®	Nightshot®
Accessory Shoe	Advanced	No	Intelligent	Intelligent
Built-in light	No	Yes	No	No
USB Interface	Yes	Yes	Yes	Yes
IEEE 1394 Interface	Yes	Yes	Yes	Yes
Microphone in port	Yes	Yes	Yes	Yes
Image Stabilization	Yes	Yes (D-EIS)	Steadyshot	Steadyshot
Pass-through Converter	Yes	No***	Yes	Yes
Weight	1lb 3oz	1lb 4oz	1lb 8oz	2lb 2oz
Life of Batter	2hrs 45min	1hr 15min	2hrs 5min	2hrs 20min
Street Price*	$570	$630	$630	$640

*Based on survey of prices available at B&H Video at www.bhphotovideo.com in December 2002
** Memory Stick
*** The Panasonic also cannot record video from an analog source such as VCR or Hi8 tapes
**** Progressive mode is for still pictures only

and Hi8 videotapes, which is an important consideration if you have an existing library of material in this format. It is equipped with high resolution, impressive zoom capabilities, megapixel still images, Nightshot, and an intelligent accessory shoe. Also, the Digital8 format uses the less-expensive Hi8 tapes for recording.

The camcorder's drawbacks are that Digital8 as a format is not on the leading edge, but rather straddles the new digital and the old analogue world. As miniDV prices come down further, the Digital8 format will be further marginalized. Digital8 camcorders are also heavier and larger than their miniDV counterparts.

DIGITAL VIDEO CONVERTERS

Digital video converters are designed to bridge the gap between your analogue VCR, Hi8, and cable TV feeds and your computer by translating the analogue signal into a digital signal that can be understood by the computer.

Most of the camcorders above have pass-through capabilities that allow them to act as analogue-to-digital converters, but lack some of the features and convenience of a converter. One feature camcorders lack is the ability to connect to a coaxial cable, which is necessary if you wish to capture content from cable TV. Another feature they lack that some converters, like the Formac Studio, have is the ability to connect to TV so that your computer can play the movie back to TV display while you are editing the movie. This is important, since video content looks very different on a TV screen than it does on a computer monitor. Dedicated converters are also convenient in that they can be connected once and left in place rather than constantly being set up and broken down, as is necessary with a pass-through system on a camcorder.

Digital converters have the added bonus of ignoring Macrovision, an antiduplication technology sometimes used in commercial VHS tapes and DVDs. Macrovision makes duplicating videos very difficult by fooling the VHS player's automatic gain control into thinking the picture is too dark or bright, tricking the VCR that is trying to make a copy of the video into overbrightening and then overdarkening the picture continuously, seriously compromising the quality of the video.

I will add that making a duplicate of a VHS tape is not illegal—you are allowed to duplicate tapes for personal use and backup copies. However, the video industry is not obligated to make that possible and uses Macrovision to compromise subsequent generations of duplications. Most digital video converters, however, ignore Macrovision and allow the computer to make uncompromised duplications of the original.

REVIEWS OF DIGITAL VIDEO CONVERTERS

Formac Studio DV/TV

As the name would have you believe, this digital video converter is tailor-made for Macs and works wonderfully (figure 9.7). It accepts inputs from almost any analogue source and will convert it to digital video. There is no configuration necessary, since Macs recognize it immediately as a legitimate digital video device.

Figure 9.7   Formac Studio DV/TV; Credit: Formac

Studio DV/TV has a coax input for both cable TV and radio antennae. You can capture content from these two inputs or use their software to turn a Mac into a TV or radio. The device can be powered by the Firewire connection to the computer, but I would suggest buying the additional $30 plug so that you can plug it into the wall; then your computer will not have to be on for it to pass video from the VCR to the TV.

Dazzle Hollywood Bridge—$260

Dazzle's Hollywood Bridge works for Macintosh or Windows computers (figure 9.8). It comes with a video editor for Windows and assumes that Mac users will use iMovie. Hollywood Bridge accepts an RCA connector from a VCR or other analogue video source and converts it to a digital signal that can be fed into your computer through the Firewire port. Unfortunately, it lacks a coax cable connector, which means that you will have to also purchase an RF Modulator (available at Radio Shack for $30) to be able to capture content from cable TV, which uses the thick, round coaxial cable.

Hollywood Bridge does have problems being recognized by iMovie sometimes and requires that you restart iMovie to reacquire the bridge for importing. I was less than impressed with its stability and tech support, which provided little assistance and was difficult to reach.

Figure 9.8   Dazzle Hollywood DV-Bridge

The Hollywood Bridge is more stable when connected to a Windows computer. Given its ability to accommodate an RF Modulator, its portability as an external device, and its low cost, the Hollywood Bridge is the unit I recommend for PCs despite the poor tech support.

Chapter Ten

Video Production Equipment

Student video productions can be facilitated by additional video equipment. This chapter will help you to understand the different pieces of equipment that are useful for student production and playback.

On the production side, a tripod or monopod is essential for capturing stable video footage. A tripod, in combination with a dolly, allows the camcorder to be rolled smoothly around a set for professional-looking video. To allow your students to properly light the set, additional lights and simple reflectors are very handy. Microphones are also useful for enhancing the sound quality of any video.

On the playback side, it is nice to have a TV that meets your needs and a DVD player that can play the movies your students have produced and burned.

PRODUCTION EQUIPMENT

Tripods

Not only is a tripod necessary for capturing smooth and stable video, it can also be a defense against damage to the camcorder. Remember that a very expensive digital camcorder with wires connecting it to the wall and microphone will be perched upon it. Therefore, it is important that the tripod be of sturdy construction. Even though the camcorders your students are likely to use will weigh less than three pounds, the tripods that are rated at 15 pounds or better are sturdier and more likely to withstand the abuse students may inflict. I have found the Velbon Videomate 607 to be

Figure 10.1   The Velbon Videomate 607

The videomate is a good example of a tripod with a fluid head, quick release, and extra triangulated leg supports.

an excellent tripod for student use. It has the best of the features listed below and a case at a reasonable price, $70 from B&H Photo and Video www.bhphotovideo.com (figure 10.1).

Tripods have different features, which are listed below.

Fluid versus Friction Heads

The head of the tripod is the part you attach to the camcorder and manipulate to pan and tilt. Fluid heads use liquid to dampen the motion and smooth the action. The alternative, friction heads, do not move as smoothly.

Quick Release

A quick release is a plate on top of the head of the tripod that you screw into the camcorder. The plate can be quickly released and reattached, for easy back and forth from tripod to handheld.

The only downside to this feature is that students frequently forget to unscrew the plate from the camcorder when they are done and return the tripod without its plate. A tripod without its quick release plate is quite useless. They sell these plates as an inexpensive accessory, but it is still a hassle to replace them. To help me remember to look for the quick release plate when students return the equipment, I list it as a separate item on the checkout sheet (figure 4.1).

Extra Leg Supports

Each leg of the tripod originates from the head and extends to the floor. Some tripods employ additional support to the legs by providing a strut for each leg in the first section that connects the legs to each other and the center pole. These struts help ensure that a leg of the tripod will not be kicked out from underneath it.

Monopods

Monopods are like tripods in that the camcorder attaches to the top of them with a screw, but monopods have only one leg that collapses (figure 10.2). The advantage of a monopod is that it does not take as long to set up and break down. It can quickly be moved and repositioned and allows for more freedom of movement than a tripod. Because there is only one leg and a simple head, it costs less than a tripod.

A monopod will help steady a camcorder, but it will not offer the same stability as a tripod and will not support a camcorder without someone

Figure 10.2   Velbon Monopod; Credit: Velbon

holding it up at all times. A monopod is not an essential piece of equipment, but rather a nice addition after you have all of the tripods you need.

Tripod Dollies

Dollies attach to the bottom of a tripod to allow the tripod to roll freely in all directions. I would encourage you to get a platform dolly that connects all the wheels together, such as the one pictured in figure 10.3, as opposed to attaching wheels to the legs of the tripod. That way the tripod legs are not stressed while rolling around but rather supported by a platform underneath. Some dollies also adjust the span of their base so that the tripod can be collapsed down to its shortest size and still fit on the dolly.

Lights

Professional-grade portable lighting sets are very costly and outside the budgets of most schools and amateur videographers. So what most of us do is settle with clip-on scoop lamps that you can buy in the hardware store (figure 10.4). Light bulbs with different wattages can provide vari-

Figure 10.3   Bogen Dolly

The dolly provides a platform on which the tripod can be rolled around a smooth surface. This tripod has expandable legs and locking pegs to stabilize it when necessary. Credit: Courtesy Bogen Photo

Figure 10.4 Portable Clip-on Lights

Simple lights such as these will provide the added light needed to properly light a video shoot. Different wattage bulbs can be used to vary the intensity of light.

ous levels of brightness, and different types of light bulbs can provide slightly different colored light.

Stands that the lights could clip onto would help position the lights, or you could just have the extra students hold them during production. Extension cords are also helpful when using lights, as the outlets never seem to be in the right place in a room.

Using additional lights will greatly improve any video production, but they are a hassle to set up and position.

Reflectors

Once again, professional-grade reflectors are outside the reach and beyond the needs of most school projects. Yet it is very useful to use a reflector to bounce natural light back onto the subject to lessen the deep shadows created by direct sunlight.

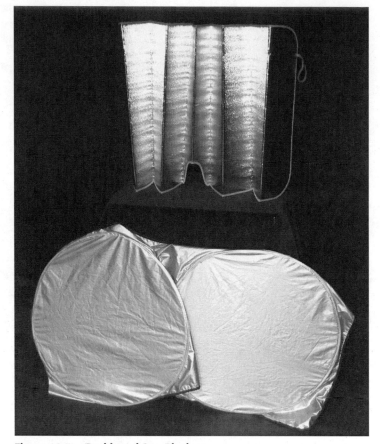

Figure 10.5   Dashboard Sun Blockers

Automobile dashboard sun blockers make decent reflectors that are inexpensive, rugged, and collapsible for easy storage.

An inexpensive and effective alternative to professional grade reflectors is to use a car dashboard sun blocker (figure 10.5). These work very well because they are durable, fold up nicely, and have a highly reflective surface.

Reflectors can greatly improve the lighting in direct sunlight conditions, as is demonstrated in figure 5.2.

Microphones

Many options exist in choosing an external microphone. For student productions, there are three basic types of microphones you may want to consider. Each microphone has a connector type and a pickup pattern.

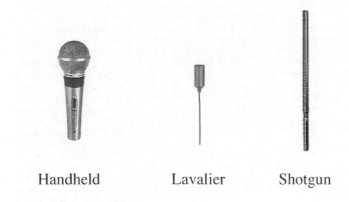

Handheld   Lavalier   Shotgun

Figure 10.6   Microphone Types

Types of Microphones (figure 10.6)

- Handheld—microphones that can be held in the hand or mounted on a stand
- Lavaliere—small microphones that can attach to clothing
- Boom—microphones attached to poles held near the action

Connectors (figure 10.7)

- Mini-phono—1/8-inch plugs used in digital video cameras and Walkmans
- Phone—1/4-inch plugs used in older stereos
- XLR—three-pinned connectors used on professional-grade microphones
- Mini-XLR—smaller versions of the XLR

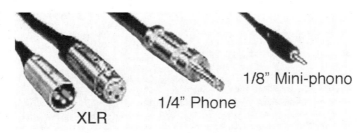

Figure 10.7   Microphone Connectors

Pickup Patterns (figure 10.8)

- Cardioid—picks up sound in front of it
- Shotgun—long, skinny mike that can record sounds from a distance
- Omnidirectional—picks up sound equally from all directions

The most useful combination of the above is a cardioid handheld microphone with a mini-phono connector. This rugged microphone will cover most
of your students' needs. The second type of microphone I recommend is an
omnidirectional lavaliere with a mini-phono connector, for more discreet microphone placements. Finally, if you have the money, a shotgun microphone
mounted on a pole, called a boom or fish pole, is a nice setup to have. It allows your students to pick up sounds from a distance, or a boom operator can
dangle the microphone just outside the field of view of the camera.

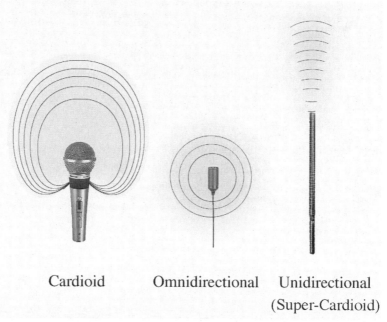

Cardioid   Omnidirectional   Unidirectional
                                   (Super-Cardioid)

Figure 10.8   Microphone Pickup Patterns

The figure above illustrates the sensitivity to sound for each pickup. The cardioid pattern is heart shaped giving it its name. The omnidirectional pattern
will pick up sounds from all directions equally. The unidirectional or super-
cardioid microphone will only pick up sound directly in front of it in a tight
pattern allowing it to pinpoint sounds from great distances.

Microphones can be connected to the camera using a cable or be wireless. If you use a cable to connect the microphone, it is useful to have a 20-foot or longer extension cable to allow for freedom of movement. Since microphones come with so many different connectors, you may also find it useful to have a collection of adapters to adapt whatever microphones you may be required to use to the 1/8-inch mini-phono port on the camera.

A wireless mike system is a wonderful luxury that will allow your students to connect any kind of microphone to the camera and not be hampered by wires. A wireless system consists of a small transmitter worn on the belt of the talent and a receiver that is plugged into the camera. Any microphone can be plugged into the transmitter, and its signal is carried via radio waves to the receiver. The drawbacks of such a system are that both the transmitter and receiver require batteries—they have an on and off switch that, if not turned off, will run the batteries down—and the system is susceptible to interference by other radio traffic.

Microphones will vary widely in cost based on their technology and impedance rating. The two types of technology are dynamic and condenser, with the dynamic being the better choice for education because it is rugged and inexpensive. As for impedance rating, the lower the better; if possible, you should try to get a microphone that is rated as 600 ohm or below, also known as low-Z. Low impedance mikes will not suffer as great a loss of quality when transmitted over long cable runs as high impedance microphones will, allowing your students to use extension cables to get the microphone close to the action.

Steadicam or Glidecam

Steadicam and Glidecam are specially designed mounts and sometimes harnesses used to steady the entire camcorder unit while a cameraperson is walking around or moving over rough terrain. These are very useful when the ground is too bumpy for a tripod and dolly (figure 10.9). However, these units cost upwards of $500, which places them outside most school budgets. Most likely your students will have to rely on their own ability to steady the camcorder and the internal image stabilization feature of the camcorder.

Figure 10.9   Steadicam JR

**The steadycam helps the cameraperson main-
tain a fluid video image while walking around
by absorbing the energy that would otherwise
shake the camcorder.**

PLAYBACK EQUIPMENT

TV Monitor

A good TV screen is important for screening the student video productions. If you have the luxury of buying a TV for screening student productions, there are some features that you will want to have. At minimum,
make sure the TV has RCA connectors for video and audio (figure 10.10).
These are the smooth round holes for RCA cables—one hole for video and
one or two holes for audio, depending on whether the TV is mono or
stereo. It is especially helpful if the TV has RCA jacks in the front for easy
access. Coax is the connector that allows you to screw the thick round
cable that carries the cable TV signal to your TV (figure 10.11). More
expensive TVs will have an S-video input as well, which is a higher-
resolution connection than the RCA or coaxial inputs. S-video is nice to
have but not totally necessary.

The proper size of the screen depends on how many people will be expected to watch the TV at any given time. When deciding how big a TV
to buy for a given audience, use the rule of thumb of one inch diagonal for
every viewer. So, for example, if your entire class of 30 students is going

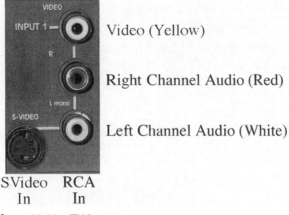

Video (Yellow)

Right Channel Audio (Red)

Left Channel Audio (White)

SVideo   RCA
In   In

Figure 10.10   TV Inputs

Figure 10.11   Coax Connector for TV

to be watching the TV at one time, your TV screen should be 30 inches diagonal.

DVD player

A DVD player is a must have if you are creating digital video content. Make sure you get one that will play all of the DVDs and VCDs you might create.

Dual Wavelength or Dual Optics

The most important feature in a DVD player is that it will play the DVD disks you have burned on your computer, which means that it will have to have dual wavelength or dual optics capabilities. Dual wavelength capabilities means that it will be able to read burned DVDs and CDs. It does not necessarily mean that it will be able to read rewritable DVDs and CDs. Make sure you use CD-R and DVD-R disks and not CD-RW and DVD-RW disks when burning your videos to disk.

There is still a DVD format war going on, so the best way to ensure that the DVDs you make will play on the DVD player you buy is to take a DVD you burned on your computer to the store to try it. This is especially true if you want to use the SVCD format described below.

Video CD (VCD) Playback

You will also want to make sure that you can view video CDs (VCDs). VCDs are a low-resolution output format that can be burned on an inexpensive CD disk as opposed to the more expensive DVD disks. DVD players that can play this format will advertise as such.

Super Video CD (SVCD) Playback

Another format you may want your DVD player to have is SVCD. This format uses low-end DVD-quality video on a regular CD disk. SVCD is not a popular format in the United States, but it could be a way to archive higher-quality video on an inexpensive CD disk, if you have a player on which to watch this format.

Progressive Scan

The progressive scan feature for DVD players is only important if your TV has progressive scan capabilities. Only digital TVs and high-end analogue TVs have progressive scan capabilities. If you have one of these TVs or expect to get one soon, it would make sense to make sure your DVD player has this feature. Progressive scan draws the entire screen at one time as opposed to drawing the screen in two passes, which allows for a sharper picture and better freeze-frame action.

Audio Options

DVD players have many audio output options. A basic player will have RCA jacks that connect your DVD player to the TV, allowing the sound to be played through the speakers on the TV (figure 10.12).

However, some DVD players are part of a home-theater system, which means that they come with five speakers and a subwoofer that plug di-

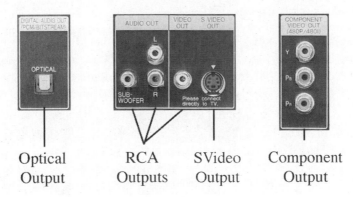

Optical   RCA   SVideo   Component

Output   Outputs   Output   Output

Figure 10.12   Output Options on DVD Players

rectly into the DVD player. These players offer the same multidimensional stereo you would experience in a theater; voices may come from one side of the screen and music from all around you. Other DVD players come with an optical port for audio that allows you to connect the DVD player to a stereo with a fiber-optic cable, so that sound quality is not compromised by signal loss over copper cables.

The home-theater and optical output options obviously cost more, and unless you have an expensive, up-to-date stereo system that accepts the optical input, or are convinced that a theater-style system is necessary, these options are not essential.

Video Out Options

DVD players use either RCA, S-Video, or BNC connectors to connect to a TV. You will notice that in figure 10.12, coax—the thick round cable with the screw-on adapter—is not an option. I have yet to see a DVD player that offers a coax out option. This is of concern because most low-end TVs do not come with RCA or S-Video inputs, which means that if you want to use these older TVs, you will have to buy an RF Modulator. Thankfully, an RF Modulator can be easily obtained at Radio Shack for about $30.

The component out option is the highest-quality connection, delivering the video signal via three separate cables, Y, P_B, P_R (figure 10.12). Only very high-end TVs and digital TVs have the inputs to accept this type of connection.

Additional Computer Hard Drives

Video consumes an enormous amount of hard drive storage space—approximately 230 MB per minute of video—with additional hard drive space needed during editing for effects, transitions, additional sound tracks, and exported movies in distribution format. Frequently, additional hard drive space will be needed as your students' projects become longer or more numerous. Luckily, adding hard drive space is not a difficult or terribly expensive proposition.

The drives you add will have to be fast enough to keep up with the speed of the video. For this you will need at least 7,200 rpm drives or faster.

Firewire Hard Drives

External Firewire hard drives are the easiest way to add hard drive space to a computer. They simply plug into the computer with the same Firewire connections used for the camera. They do, however, use the larger six-pin connectors at both ends of the cable, as opposed to the camcorders that use the smaller four-pin to six-pin cable.

Because Firewire is a standard, no drivers or software are needed to make use of Firewire drives. At the most, you may have to format the drive the first time it is used.

The portability of the external drives is an added bonus. I sometimes sign out the Firewire drives to a group of students for the duration of a project. They are able to store their project on the drive and plug it into any computer in the lab that is free. When they are finished for the day, they can unplug the drive and return it to the storage closet for safekeeping. When they are done working on their project, they can plug the drive with their finished product into the one computer that has the DVD burner on it and burn their project to a DVD.

I will raise a word of caution about the integrity of these devices, however. If a Firewire hard drive is not properly dismounted from the computer before it is unplugged, you risk losing all the data on the disk. On the Mac side, dismounting the drive means dragging the drive to the trash can or shutting down the computer. On the PC side, it means logging out or shutting down. I have had students lose many hours of work when a drive was unplugged while it was transferring data to the computer. To protect students from losing everything on especially important projects, it is always a good idea to periodically export the movie in progress back to the camera for backup.

Internal Hard Drives

Internal hard drives are less expensive than external drives because the manufacturer does not have to build in a power supply or external casing. They also are not as susceptible to losing all their data because of dismounting problems and are more reliable than the external Firewire drives, in my experience.

Installing an internal drive is more complicated than installing an external Firewire drive because you have to open the computer and connect the drive to the internal power source and data cable. Adding an internal hard drive is within the capabilities of anyone willing to give it a try and follow the directions.

Network Server or Network Hard Drive

Using network storage space for video is generally a bad idea. Moving the amount of data required for video over a network will severely tax the average school network and will usually give unsatisfactory results. At this point in time, local hard drives are the preferred storage device for video.

Chapter Eleven

Media Literacy and Teaching Evaluation of Media Content

Media literacy, according to the Center for Media Literacy, is "The ability to communicate competently in all media forms, print and electronic, as well as to access, understand, analyze and evaluate the powerful images, words and sounds that make up our contemporary mass media culture" (www.medialit.org, 3/31/2002). While most of this book focuses on teaching students to "communicate" in video format, it is also very important that students be able to "analyze and evaluate" powerful media messages. Our students are deluged with mass media messages, and educating them about how to evaluate these media messages will diminish their influence. Students will learn the ways in which the media manipulates their feelings, influences their thinking, inspires and defines their culture, and dictates their fashions.

Plato's shadows on the cave wall are today's TV, movies, and other media outlets. A powerful marketing industry has been attempting to target our students' interests and shape their preferences since they were old enough to watch TV or go to Chuck-e-Cheese. As teens, our students become huge consumers of mass media, watching an average of 23 hours of television per week, or 1,500 hours a year, compared with the 900 hours they will spend per year in the classroom (*Media Smart*). Since students spend that much time transfixed by the TV, marketers have been highly successful in creating an unending appetite for commercial goods. They lure our students by presenting an extremely attractive, if imaginary, world filled with beautiful people and enormous wealth. The students need to know that what they see promoted on TV and at the movies is not representative of the real world and is sometimes counter to their best interests.

One of the earliest and most successful advertising campaigns in our country convinced our society that for women to smoke was not only acceptable but desirable. Cigarettes were labeled "torches of freedom" after World War II, and advertisements quoted movie star Constance Talmadge saying, "*Light a Lucky* and you'll never miss sweets that make you fat" (Gourley 1999, 48, 50). Even today, the advertising industry touts bone-thin models and manipulates pictures to make them even thinner, promoting an unrealistic body image our students may try to emulate in unhealthy ways. It is imperative that our students be made aware of the fact that TV is not real life and that their definition of beauty is being defined by an industry interested in selling them products.

Advertising is not always easy to spot. It has become sophisticated, subtle, and so tightly woven into almost all media content it is sometimes difficult to identify. Product placement in movies and TV shows promotes brand names in an almost subliminal way. It is not by chance that Ethan Hunt used a Macintosh laptop in the movie *Mission Impossible*. Apple paid substantially from its marketing budget to place that product in the hands of Tom Cruise, in hopes that impressionable teens and young adults would associate Macintosh computers with the glamorous world of secret agents. Sports figures are paid huge sums of money to wear manufacturers' shoes and other apparel. Movie stars are given expensive clothing and accessories to promote a look and its designer.

In addition to promoting commercial products, marketers also help politicians construct personas, craft campaigns, and launch public relation initiatives to win support for their proposals. Spin doctors—paid consultants who act as marketers—attempt to interpret events and influence the thinking of the public in the way most advantageous to their clients.

What is most important for students to understand is that all media messages are constructed by people for a purpose. Students must understand that every message has a motive, and ascertaining what that motive is will help students become active, critical viewers (Hobbs 2000, H-5). Students should ask the following five questions about any media message:

1. Who created this message?
2. What is the purpose of this message?

3. What techniques are used to attract and hold attention?
4. What point of view is presented in this message?
5. What has been left out of this message? (*Media Smart*)

When students begin to ask these questions about the messages they receive from programs, commercials, newscasts, movies, and other media, they will become more discerning about, and therefore less influenced by, poorly thought out or biased media messages.

WHO CREATED THIS MESSAGE?

Is the creator a reputable service organization interested in public safety or a marketing firm interested in selling something? If it is a marketing firm, it is also important for students to know that these are frequently outsourced services. Most companies do not make their own commercials, preferring instead to hire an advertising or marketing firm to construct a strategy designed to create a public desire for the product(s).

Is the creator of the message an organization? If so, what is the mission of the organization and bias? Messages created by the organization will be in keeping with the mission statement and colored by its bias. Sometimes the mission statement will reveal the bias, such as the Republican National Committee's commitment to promoting Republican candidates in elections. Clearly, messages from this committee would be pro-Republican and represent a conservative bias.

News organizations are the subject of a national debate over the "liberal bias in the media." Their mission is to inform the public, but some subscribers claim that they do so with a liberal bias. This is an overly simplistic view of the news media. The truth is that news media outlets run the spectrum from ultraliberal to ultraconservative. My local newspaper tends to favor the conservative viewpoint, while the regional paper advocates a more liberal interpretation. *U.S. News & World Report* is more conservative than *Time*, and ABC's *World News Tonight* is more liberal than *Fox News*, and so on.

Is the creator an individual and, if so, what is his or her personal bias? Each person has his or her own perception of reality, the result of factors as diverse as religious beliefs, personal experience, environment, and even genetic composition. Once the creator of the message is identified, if possible, have the students determine the bias or agenda of that person or organization. Determining the bias will give the students insight into the creator's motivation. For this reason, students need to be taught to consider who created the message when processing the information contained within it.

WHAT IS THE PURPOSE OF THIS MESSAGE?

Is the purpose of the message to inform, entertain, persuade, or sell something? Most often a message will contain elements of all four. TV news organizations, for example, whose purpose is to inform, are also trying to entertain to attract a large audience, and in a sense are selling you their show and their representation of the news. News programs run the spectrum from highly informative programming with no commercials and little flair—such as public TV's *Newshour with Jim Lehrer,* which contains extended discussions with experts representing multiple perspectives—to shows like NBC's *Dateline,* which reports sensationalized news to attract the largest possible audience, so that the network can charge more money for the advertisements aired during the show. Sometimes a news show will emphasize entertainment at the expense of accuracy, as happened in *Dateline*'s investigative report on a General Motors truck with a certain type of gas tank that was said to explode during side impact crashes. *Dateline* wanted to show footage of a simulated crash resulting in an explosion. When their first two attempts to create the deadly scenario failed, they rigged the gas cap to pop off on impact and ignited the spilled gas with a toy rocket under the rear fender (Gourley 1999, 19). *Dateline* clearly crossed the line between reporting and misrepresenting reality and was sued by General Motors as a result. The motivation for concocting this scenario was to create a visually exciting news story with high entertainment value to attract a large audience, even if it did not represent reality.

Sometimes a show whose primary purpose is to entertain will also have a political agenda. Take NBC's very popular show *The West Wing,* which dramatizes life in the White House through the vantage point of a Democratic president and his staff. This highly entertaining show clearly champions the Democratic party line and frequently dramatizes actual contemporary political events and situations. Having students identify the purpose of the message forces them to assess the message and move to a level of intellectual, not just emotional, response.

WHAT TECHNIQUES ARE USED TO ATTRACT AND HOLD ATTENTION?

How is the content portrayed through video? Video makers have amazing control over the medium and have learned how to elicit visceral reactions to video images. They decide where the camera is relative to the subject, what is in the picture, what colors are used, how the camera and subject move, what is said, what music is used, how well lighted the picture is, and so on. While you are watching a video, the video maker controls everything you see and hear. Many different techniques are used in video to get and hold your attention. The booming voice of an announcer yelling about a monster truck rally at the speedway over the sounds of roaring vehicles and smashing glass is an intentional use of loud noises to get the attention of the viewer and capture the destructive, raucous, and entertaining nature of the event. The fast-paced pop music of Britney Spears and the choreographed moves of a group of attractive dancers are an intentional use of music and sex appeal to get the attention of potential Pepsi consumers.

Video techniques do not have to be as obvious as loud announcers, suggestive dances, and teen idols. Very subtle techniques are used with equal effectiveness. A camera angle shift can totally change your view of a subject. In the movie *Ruthless People,* Danny DeVito, who is five foot one, was rarely shown from above in order to conceal his true height. In one particular scene, the camera operator shot DeVito from a low angle and a shorter than normal telephone booth is used so that when DeVito picked up the receiver, he does not have to reach up to get it. The low camera angle and shortened props make DeVito look taller.

In addition to camera angles, colors used in a video are carefully chosen. When video makers are trying to be dramatic, they often use black or darker colors as their predominant color. Even politicians carefully choose the color tie they wear in public: the aggressive, bold, "power" tie is red; the more gentle and sensitive tie is blue.

If students come to understand that these techniques are being used to get their attention and create a desired reaction, they will be better able to separate the product or information from the techniques used to attract their interest and manipulate their emotions. They may also begin to decode the messages of mass media and the marketing wizards and tap into the subtle uses of video for emotional effect. The subject is discussed further in chapter 3.

WHAT POINT OF VIEW IS PRESENTED IN THIS MESSAGE?

People interpret events differently based on their role in any given situation. For example, a doctor is going to view a diagnosis or medical procedure differently from a patient, just as a defendant is going to view a trial differently from a prosecutor.

Students should understand that stories are related from a point of view. In each message, students should identify whose perspective is being represented and then take into account the bias that person may bring to the story.

WHAT HAS BEEN LEFT OUT OF THIS MESSAGE?

Sometimes this is the most difficult and important question to ask. A message can be factually correct, yet misleading if it is taken out of context or if some details are simply omitted. This becomes even more of a problem if the viewer lacks general knowledge in this area, giving the creator of the message a greater ability to manipulate the message. It is the responsibility of the viewer to realize that information not presented can drastically affect the integrity of a message. A well-balanced report on a subject will be careful to represent all sides equally. A report that does not do so constitutes a biased message that the students should treat with skepticism.

WILLING SUSPENSION OF DISBELIEF

Much of our ability to enjoy movies and TV is predicated on our "willing suspension of disbelief." This is our ability to turn off our innate skepticism, practical knowledge of real life, and understanding of the laws of physics so that we can be entertained by unrealistic events and sensationalized stories. Students need to be aware that they do this when they are being entertained. They should also be taught not to do this when consuming all media messages.

As they critically evaluate media using the five questions above, and when they begin to produce their own videos, students will begin to recognize the shadows on the cave wall for what they are. I have had students tell me that they will never be able to look at video the same way again; their minds are busy identifying the purpose of the video, isolating the biases of the creator, analyzing the techniques of the director, and archiving video effects for emulation in their next video creations.

FURTHER INFORMATION ABOUT MEDIA LITERACY

Media literacy is becoming increasingly important as media messages become more sophisticated and numerous. The study of media literacy can be integrated into almost any discipline at every level. Many excellent resources exist to assist you further in developing a media literacy curriculum to complement your existing curriculum (see especially www.medialit.org).

Appendix

VIDEO SCAVENGER HUNT TASKS

Videotape as many of the following events as possible to achieve the highest score

Try to buy something at the bookstore with a foreign currency	100
Find a twin for every member of the team	75
Bonus for best look-alike	100
Ask students what they want to do with their life	35
Impersonate your favorite rock star	50
Perform as barbershop quartet with choreography	50
Ask non-team members to name the 13 original colonies,	
and the one they would vote off the island	50
Kiss a fish	35
Change clothes with other team members	30
Breakdance on a cardboard box in public	175
Bonus for each move	75
Bonus for getting stranger to join in	50
Point at nothing and get passerby to look at it	50
Video an animal	30
Bonus for finding more than three species	75
Get someone on your team to sing and act out the teapot song	50
Have someone on your team defend him or herself from	
attackers using martial arts	50
Comment on a student's behavior as if narrating a nature program	75
Travel the halls as if you were The Crocodile Hunter in the wild	75

Create an obstacle on a sidewalk and then act as Olympic judges, rating how well passersby navigate it	40
Take a nap in an inappropriate location	35
Re-enact the "King of the World" scene from Titanic	30
Get in a car "Dukes of Hazard" style	30
Film an opposing team member standing still for more than 10 seconds	50
In a public area, give your best impersonation of a pro wrestler's pre-fight interview	50
Interview people coming out of a rest room	50
Video a team member acting like a duck	5/per
Play an air badminton game in public	40
Video a team member climbing a tree	15
Video team members playing leap frog	15
Scoring a goal on the green and doing your best end-zone dance	75
Video a team member dunking a basketball	75
Serenade the principal	75
Recite a poem publicly	50
Bonus if you make up your own and strangers stop to listen	50
Have every member of your team hop a fence	35
Come up with a rock paper scissors game for your whole team and demonstrate how it works	50
Capture team members lovingly running towards each other across a field	50
Video a team becoming part of one of Mr. Love's classes	75
Bonus if you can supplant the teacher and continue teaching	150
Ride in the maintenance cart	125
Have a formal meal in the dining hall	75
Bonus for candles	25
Enact a dramatic finish to a running race between team members	50

CAMERA AND BATTERY CARE INSTRUCTIONS

Camera Care

Handle Camcorder with care!
DO NOT:
Drop
Expose to water
Leave in your car
Leave unattended
Point camcorder at the sun
Point viewfinder or LCD at the sun
Pick up camcorder by viewfinder

DO:
Acclimate camcorder before use (Make sure camcorder and tape are the
 same temperature as climate in which they are being used)
Use only infoLITHIUM batteries
Recharge battery before you return
Use power adapter whenever possible
Read manual for advanced features
Make sure to remove your tape when returned

Reminder:
You are responsible for any damage, loss, or theft of equipment
while in your care.

* * * * *

Battery Care

Battery
The Battery will last about:
 40 min with viewfinder
 30 min with LCD display

Recharge time: Approx. 2 Hours

Recharge the battery before you return
Turn power off
Plug in Camcorder with battery installed
Read LCD display on side
Leave plugged in 1 hour past Full

Reminder:
You are responsible for any damage, loss, or theft of equipment while in your care.

SAMPLE RELEASE FORM

Talent Release Form:

Date: _____

I _____

Residing at: _____
               Street   City   State   Zip

hereby give (*name of school or production team*) permission to use, pictures, video images, and audio recordings of me for broadcasting and exhibition as part of (*name of production*).

I hereby release you from any claims arising out of, or resulting from, my appearance and my statements in the above production.

Signature: Guardian's Signature:
                                          (If above is less than 18)

_____   _____

Print Name: Print Name:

_____   _____

Date: Date:

_____   _____

Bibliography

Adams, Dennis, and Mary Hamm. 1989. *Media and Literacy, Learning in an Electronic Age—Issues, Ideas, and Teaching Strategies*. Chicago: Charles C Thomas.

Adams, Dennis, and Mary Hamm. 2000. *Media and Literacy, Learning in an Electronic Age—Issues, Ideas, and Teaching Strategies*. 2nd ed. Chicago: Charles C Thomas.

Adler, Stella. 1988. *The Technique of Acting*. Toronto: Bantam.

Anglin, Gary J., ed. 1995. *Instructional Technology, Past, Present, and Future*. 2nd ed. Englewood, Colo.: Libraries Unlimited.

Brown, James A. 1991. *Television "Critical Viewing Skills" Education: Major Media Literacy Projects in the United States and Selected Countries*. Hillsdale, N.J.: Lawrence Erlbaum.

Bunch, John B. 1986. "Educational Media and Aesthetic Education." *Journal of Aesthetic Education* 20, no. 3 (Fall).

Bunch, John B. 1990. "Professional Advice on Videotaping Instruction." *Performance and Instruction* (January).

Bunch, John B. 1996. "Video for Photographers" *The Focal Encyclopedia of Photography*. New York: Focal Press.

Burrows, Thomas D., Lynne S. Gross, James C. Foust, and Donald N. Wood. 2001. *Video Production: Disciplines and Techniques*. 8th ed. Boston: McGraw-Hill.

Compesi, Ronald J. 2000. *Video Field Production and Editing*. 5th ed. Boston: Allyn and Bacon.

Cook, Jeff Scott. 1989. *The Elements of Speechwriting and Public Speaking*. New York: Macmillan.

Davies, John. 1996. *Educating Students in a Media-Saturated Culture*. Lancaster, Pa.: Technomic.

Gourley, Catherine. 1999. *Media Wizards*. Brookfield, Conn.: Twenty-First Century Books.

Hampe, Barry. 1997. *Making Documentary Films and Reality Videos: A Practical Guide to Planning, Filming, and Editing Documentaries of Real Events*. New York: Henry Holt.

Harrop, John and Sabin R. Epstein. 1982. *Acting with Style*. Upper Saddle River, N.J.: Prentice Hall.

Herrell, Adrienne L., and Joel P. Fowler Jr. *Camcorder in the Classroom*. Upper Saddle River, N.J.: Prentice Hall, 1998.

Hobbs, Renee. 2000. *Assignment: Media Literacy*. Bethesda, Md.: Discovery Communications, Inc.

Kaplan, Don. 1980. *Video in the Classroom*. White Plains, N.Y.: Knowledge Industry Publications.

Kennedy, Robert. 2001. *Teaching TV Production in a Digital World: Integrating Media Literacy*. Englewood, Colo.: Libraries Unlimited.

Kyker, Keith, and Christopher Curchy. 1994. *Television Production for Elementary School*. Englewood, Colo.: Libraries Unlimited.

LeBaron, John. 1981. *Making Television: A Video Production Guide for Teachers*. New York: Teachers College Press.

Leeds, Dorothy. 1988. *Powerspeak: The Complete Guide to Persuasive Public Speaking and Presenting*. New York: Prentice Hall.

Limpus, Bruce. 1994. *Lights, Camera, Action! A Guide to Using Video Production and Instruction in the Classroom*. Waco, Tex.: Prufrock Press.

Media Smart: A Media Literacy Project from WETA. Arlington, Va.: Public TV 26, [1][n.d.].

Millerson, Gerald. 2001. *Video Production Handbook*. 3rd ed. Boston: Focal Press.

Schramm, Wilbur Lang. 1977. *Big Media Little Media*. Newbury Park, Calif.: Sage Publications.

Seattler, Paul. 1990. *The Evolution of American Educational Technology*. Englewood, Colo.: Libraries Unlimited.

The Center for Media Literacy. "The Center for Media Literacy—Empowerment through Education." Hp. Available URL: www.medialit.org (3/31/2002).

Vassallo, Wanda. 1990. *Speaking with Confidence: A Guide for Public Speakers*. White Hall, Va.: Betterway Publications.

York, Matt, ed. 2001. *The Computer Videomaker Handbook*. Boston: Focal Press.

Index

About the Author

Dan Greenwood has been involved in integrating technology into education for over ten years. He began his career in education as a middle school teacher of social studies, math, and computers at St. Paul's School in Clearwater, Florida. Recognizing the power and potential of computer technology in education, he sought formal training in computer and networking technology and received his certified network administrator and certified network engineer credentials. Through the Florida Council of Independent School (FCIS), Dan established the FCIS SchoolNet, a statewide e-mail and conferencing network.

Greenwood then moved to Richmond, Virginia, to become the director of technology at St. Catherine's School, where he facilitates further development of the technology program, providing leadership and training. He is responsible for the direction and implementation of a technology program to complement and enhance the existing educational program and curriculum.

He has held leadership roles in the Virginia Association of Independent Schools as the technology chair for the Professional Development Committee and as a member of the Technology Steering Committee. He also founded and ran two different week-long technology seminars and workshops on implementing technology in education.

Greenwood is currently seeking his master of education from the University of Virginia in Instructional Technology. He presents at many conferences and enjoys sharing his experiences and knowledge with other educators.